Child Custody A to Z

Child Custody A to Z

Winning with Evidence

Guy J. White

iUniverse, Inc.

New York Lincoln Shanghai

Child Custody A to Z
Winning with Evidence

iUniverse books may be ordered through booksellers or by contacting:

iUniverse
2021 Pine Lake Road, Suite 100
Lincoln, NE 68512
www.iuniverse.com
1-800-Authors (1-800-288-4677)

ISBN: 0-595-33656-6

Printed in the United States of America

Contents

Legal Disclaimer

All those involved in publishing this book have done their best to provide useful and accurate information. However, this book does not take the place of a lawyer, private investigator, or mental health professional.

This book does not cover the laws of any particular state. It only provides the most basic and general knowledge of concepts and ideas about custody. The legal principles have been simplified to make the material easier to understand by the general public.

If you want or need specific advice, please seek the counsel of an appropriate professional familiar with the laws in your state. There is no guarantee of accuracy expressed or implied, and the explanatory sections of this book are not be considered as legal advice or a restatement of law.

While every effort has been made to ensure that this book's information is up to date and accurate, mistakes in content and typography may have been made.

Foreword

The sun is beginning to hide behind the desert mountain as I draw my Smith & Wesson .357 from my pull-through Alessi holster. I punch the weapon forward, find the front sight, and pop three rounds—two to the body and one to the head.

Unfortunately, it's time to go. Another Saturday evening that won't be mine. I holster my weapon and throw away my paper target. Tonight I have a new target. She's blonde and the battle is child custody. She's 29 and having an affair with a professional football player. My assignment is to document her lifestyle.

My weapons will be a video camera and a notebook. She's partying in Tempe, Arizona, tonight at a local pub. I know it well because I've watched her there several times before. She'll drive up in her sporty BMW and drink the night away. I'll follow her wherever she goes. If she goes home, I'll write down the license plate of the babysitter so I can interview her later. If there is no babysitter, I'll write that down as well.

Seven months later, I sat in the courtroom as the judge interviewed the woman. I'll never forget when he asked her, "Ma'am, how does every other Sunday sound?"

"Excuse me, Your Honor, I don't understand the question," she said.

"Ma'am, I am ordering the visitation schedule for you to visit your children."

"Visitation schedule? she asked, the judge's words still not registering.

"Yes, Ma'am, your husband is awarded sole custody and I want to know if every other Sunday for visitation will coincide with your schedule."

Every other Sunday and no overnight visitation is pretty severe. This is an example of goal setting and evidence collection coming together for a common cause. I am the middleman between success and failure. I am the investigator who documents, motivates, and sees the client through an emotional event. I liberate children from bad parents.

I was told later the mother wanted to kill me. She'll just have to wait in line with the rest. The father listened to his attorney and me and he prevailed. You can, too.

This book is dedicated to educating people about the nuts and bolts of child custody and how the battles are lost and won.

Introduction

The concepts and cases presented in this book are from day-to-day accounts of the war zone called **child custody**. This book is the product of 20 years of experience I have gained from cases I have personally worked. The people will remain anonymous except for the high profile cases or ones of national significance. Some of it might seem over the top, but the drama and anecdotes are sometimes necessary to show the impact of these emotional and sometimes deadly battles.

As a forensic investigator, I wrote this book to explain the gap that is prevalent in the legal system. The art and techniques of gathering evidence is the theme of this book. However, I also show the importance of tactics and strategy. I'm not trying to make you a first-class sleuth. I'm simply showing you how to navigate through a flawed justice system.

With an ever-increasing divorce rate in America, the broken family has put our children at risk. To say one parent is better than another can only be examined on a case-by-case basis. Some mothers are bad parents and so are some fathers. I didn't write this book to teach dirty tricks to wannabe parents. Quite the contrary, this book is a manual to expose the truth in a broken and overwhelmed justice system.

I have seen parents in circumstances few attorneys, psychologists, or judges ever witness. Because I have seen people at their worst, I have endured more than most therapists. So I apologize for what might seem like a cold approach. The fact is I go through much of the hell my clients do. I see inside their lives and see what they really are.

I have prevented kidnappings, suicides, and murders, and I have made every effort to work for clients who will serve their child's best interests. Sometimes this is difficult. Anyone can be fooled. Consequently, I put my potential clients through an interview or interrogation only a few attorneys would try.

This book includes case studies that support my techniques. Furthermore, it is my hope that by reading this book you will learn something that will help you win your child a better life.

I

Custody

The Combat Mindset

A mistake many parents make in custody fights is to let their anger control their behavior. Consequently, they may do something that could affect their relationship with their child for many years. Control in a stressful situation is critical to success.

Stop whining! You must control your emotions if you are going to win custody. You must think clearly and concisely and put your emotions aside. I know this is easier said than done. It reminds me of two boxers in the ring. One boxer loses his temper and forgets all his training. The other boxer remains poised and demolishes his opponent.

The same is true in child custody. A lot of people make all of their decisions based on emotion rather than logic. People do this every day in custody cases, which is why many of them lose. Of course, there's also the population of people who don't have the stomach to deal with difficult situations. These people fail their children every day because they lack the courage to do the right thing—to set a goal and follow through.

I COMMANDMENT
CONTROL YOUR EMOTIONS

Without controlling your emotions you may fail. If you think about the decisions you made under stress or heavy emotion, they were usually bad decisions. If you control your emotions, you can think clearer and make better decisions. I have recommended to my clients many times to seek counseling while going through a custody battle. The counselor may help you work out your frustration, hostility, and trauma during this difficult time. Once you have worked out the trauma, you can prepare for your custody battle and put the welfare of your child first and foremost.

Custody, like any objective or obstacle, must be approached the same way you do business. You must first set the goal, then you must determine what it will take to accomplish the goal, including forming and performing a plan of action. People do this all the time as part of their business lives, but when it involves their children they forget everything they ever learned about goal setting or mission statements.

It's the same in child custody battles. Of course, you probably just hired a hotshot lawyer who's going to chase the monsters away and make everything okay. You know this is true, because you just paid them a lot of money. If you are a mother, your attorney might tell you that you will get child support and the father will get limited visitation. If you are a father, you might be told you'll pay child support because you have no chance of getting custody. *But it's a myth mothers always win custody!*

Don't let the legal community lie to you. I know. I have dealt with this in my own family. We went to five so-called top-flight attorneys. They all said the same thing. "You don't have a chance." They said we would be lucky to know the child by the time he's five years old. But we won sole custody when the child was only 15 months old. In my opinion, in our case the mother set the trap of marriage by getting pregnant—without a doubt the oldest trick in the book. Unfortunately, it still works on a lot of people, but in this case not only did it fail, but it backfired. Here's how:

1. We were committed to winning.

2. We controlled our emotions, thus improving our thought processes.

3. We found the best people to help us—attorneys, investigators, and so on.

4. We relied on ourselves—not the system—to prevail.

5. We were willing to admit our weaknesses or vulnerabilities.

Commitment is absolutely vital to winning custody. And the more help you can enlist to achieve the goal of custody the better.

As I said earlier, you must **control your emotions** regardless of the events. Sometimes there may be kidnappings, arrests, accidents, or suicide attempts. Your spouse may yank the children out of one school and enroll them in another. Whatever the circumstances are, *you must stay in control.*

Good advice is tantamount to winning your custody case. Naturally, having the best people work with you is going to improve your attitude. And having a good attitude is going to help your emotional health.

Throughout this book I'll continue to make the point that the system is imperfect or just plain stinks. That's why **self-reliance** is so important. You will have to actively get involved in your case to ensure the system works.

Every play in football is designed to score a touchdown. But how many touchdowns are scored per game compared to the number of plays run? In the legal system, few attorneys bother to formulate a plan that will score a legal touchdown. First of all, the playing field is biased—meaning the judge may not like you or your gender. There are an almost infinite number of things that can go wrong in your case. You may have a bad lawyer, judge, or psychologist. As a result of this incompetence, failure may be imminent. Again, self-reliance can temper or even prevent the worst of circumstances. If you have the knowledge and weapons, you might just avoid becoming a losing statistic.

It is critical to your case to know your strengths and weaknesses. While admitting weaknesses or vulnerabilities can be very difficult, identifying them will help you to improve your position. With each of my clients, I analyze, evaluate, and help make changes when necessary. Still, people tend to hear what they want to hear.

This **cognitive dissonance** has a catastrophic effect on a person's case when a court appointed psychologist interviews them to determine who the custodial parent will be. If the parent lacks the ability to focus on their problems or shortcomings, their parenting skills might be affected. If the parent is doing something wrong or ineffective regarding their parenting, the psychologist may take a hard line on the parent's denial.

Another hazard that plagues parents is burdening their children with the animosity toward the other parent. An example would be a parent taking out their frustration for the other parent on the children. One parent often talks bad about the other to the children thus undermining the relationship the children have with that parent. This is an emotional response to their divorce or custody case and can be a real setback because psychologists don't take this lightly. I explain this scenario more in "The Case of the Murdered Fiancée" in Part I.

How you think may separate winning from losing in a custody case. I can't tell you how many times a parent has said to me their spouse would "never do something evil." If you judge your opponent with your value system, you are setting yourself up for failure because your opponent most likely has a different value system. Just because you may not seek revenge doesn't mean your opponent won't. When battling for custody I have seen people do all kinds of things, including murder. You simply cannot believe a parent is not capable of evil acts perpetrated on you or your child.

II COMMANDMENT
NEVER UNDERESTIMATE YOUR OPPONENT

Too many times I have had a parent tell me their spouse would never accuse them of child molestation or some other heinous crime—and they were wrong. You can never underestimate what a parent will do when they are fighting over their child. During a divorce or custody battle people are at their worst. I have seen kidnapping, murder, and unbelievable accusations during a custody battle. Don't assume a parent is not dangerous or vindictive during a nasty custody battle.

Sometimes you have to hope for the best but prepare for the worst. You may even need to anticipate evil behavior so you can counter your opponent's effort. For example, many people have violent confrontations during visitation exchanges. One parent may use abusive language in front of the child, or a parent may have a girlfriend or boyfriend who is abusive during these exchanges. If so, the confrontation needs to be video or audio taped to preserve this evidence in your case.

I've been accused of being paranoid or anal, but I have good reasons for my attitude. It's the attention to details that determines who wins. I have risked my life in my business as well as in military operations, and I know the consequences of not being prepared. If your parachute is not packed properly, you may die. If you are a pilot and you don't check your fuel gauge, you may die.

Some people just don't have the presence of mind to check the important details before they take on a mission. Every year, people drown because they are unprepared or simply cannot swim. Every year, people die in the desert because they don't have enough water. Your custody case is no different. If you are not prepared, your chances of losing are good. In the courtroom, details are very important. So the way you think is vital to winning. You need an attorney who knows that being prepared is the key to winning. Being prepared means all the relevant details of your case are applied. These people have the combat mindset and they understand details and tactics.

Anatomy of Child Custody

Most child custody cases begin with divorce. Divorce seems to bring out the worst in people like nothing else. During a divorce, each parent often hires their own attorney. At that point, one or both of the parents may decide they want sole custody. Generally, the definition of **sole custody** is that the child will live with one parent most of the time, and this parent will make decisions on the child's life, such as what school the child will attend. The **custodial parent**, that is, the parent who is awarded sole custody by the judge in a court of law, has the power to make decisions regarding the child's life. Typically, a **non-custodial parent**, or parent without sole custody, has no decision-making rights regarding the child.

If custody is to be decided in a court of law, a judge is going to make the decision because the parents cannot agree. Each parent will have an attorney and the judge will often appoint a psychologist to make an unbiased study of the family to determine which parent should have sole custody or whether joint custody would be better for the child.

Often psychologists will recommend **joint custody**. Joint custody is where both parents have equal decision-making power over the child. However, this doesn't mean the parents have equal *time* with the child.

The other option is **joint physical custody**, in which both parents share the child equally and they both have input into the child's life. This means each parent will get the children about 50 percent of the time.

The other distinction is **physical custody**. This means the children will live with one parent most of the time, who is then the **primary parent**. The visitation schedule may vary depending on the psychologist's recommendation.

Essentially, the children will have a primary residence. This is one of the beefs fathers have. They agree to joint custody but in reality, if the mother gets physical custody, they receive a disproportionate time with the children. So, in this situation a label may not mean anything. In a perfect world, joint custody can work if parents get equal time. (Unfortunately, we don't live in a perfect world, which is why you are reading this book.) If parents could get along and agree and know what is best for their children, then joint custody would work.

I sometimes don't believe in joint custody because nothing gets accomplished when parents have equal power, particularly when they don't get along. I have seen parents in court years later squabbling over parochial school versus public school or Little League versus tennis. This bickering can get ridiculous.

When parents fight for custody, the judge usually appoints a psychologist. The judge considers the psychologist an expert witness and an expert on parents. Generally, the judge will award custody based on the psychologist's evaluation of the parents. The psychologist will perform a **family study**, an examination of the parents to determine their lifestyle, philosophy on life, and their ability to raise children. The family study tests parenting skills and personality types. Often the psychologist will determine who gets what based on the personality type of the parent. I will go over this evaluation and what it means later in Part 4.

There are many variations regarding custody. Some parents agree on the primary care of the child, but they don't agree on custody. While custody is just a word, in an adversarial justice system, labels can mean a lot to parents and their egos.

Parents generally overrate labels. A lot of parents boast about having sole custody. But each parent has visitation rights. So, if a parent doesn't have sole custody, he still has the right to visit his child. These are legal concerns, and your attorney in your state can explain to you what your visitation rights are. Some parents ask the judge or the court for a change of custody years after their divorce. Where divorce is permanent, custody is not. Custody can be changed or amended almost anytime. And the same scenario will occur with regard to the anatomy of the case. The only difference is the emotional and financial burden of the divorce will most likely not be present.

The judge makes all the decisions in custody when the parents cannot agree on the care of the children. But remember, the judge appoints a psychologist to determine who should raise the child. Again, generally speaking, the judge will determine custody through the recommendation of the psychologist nearly all the time, though I have seen exceptions.

Some attorneys agree ahead of time to living with the results of the evaluation of the psychologist to prevent a trial. I personally think this is a bad idea because circumstances can change on a daily basis. I don't believe it is good judgment to agree to anything because nobody knows what the future will bring.

In the event your case goes to trial, you will need to put on your case. Your attorney will need to interview or subpoena witnesses on your behalf to show and prove you are the better parent. Of course, this can be expensive, but it is necessary in cases where the parents cannot agree on the important issues.

Attorneys will sometimes call character witnesses who will testify on your behalf. Bear in mind that a case that goes to trial will take a long time. The court system is slow, broken down, and overworked. The upside is this time can be used to prepare your case.

Three Ways to Win Custody

There are three ways for you to win custody:

1. Win over the psychologist

2. Win over the judge

3. Win over the psychologist *and* the judge

Now that you understand that the psychologist generally makes the primary decision for custody and the judge makes the final decision on custody, you need to know how to win. As I have said before, you need to win over the psychologist. Sometimes this just is not possible. Psychologists are just people and they bring their own biases to their profession. Some psychologists are biased toward mothers, while some are biased toward fathers.

Parents often will try to win over the court-appointed psychologist with sweet talk. They often will try to "buddy up" to them to convince the psychologist they are the best parent for the child. Sometimes this strategy works. But often the psychologist sees through this. That's why I say over and over in this book the best way to win custody is with **evidence**—the most overlooked element of custody. Lawyers and psychologists are neither trained investigators nor interrogators. They are victims of their education.

If your evidence is solid, the psychologist should award a favorable recommendation to you, though this isn't always the case. The reason, again, is because some psychologists are biased, I have worked on cases when we had good evidence against the opposing parent and the psychologist accused us of being petty. There are two reasons for this:

1. The psychologist is burned out and no amount of evidence impresses them.

2. The psychologist has never seen a parent so prepared regarding their case.

Some psychologists just haven't been exposed to a carefully prepared investigation of the facts. And sometimes they resent your aggressive and thorough preparation. But the alternative of not being prepared is worse.

Sometimes you feel like you just can't win. You are prepared and your facts paint a grim picture of your spouse. The psychologists just might be upset that your investigation is so comprehensive that they are embarrassed they didn't uncover the facts like you did. Psychologists are so-called "experts" and they do not like to look stupid. So their egos sometimes get in the way of the facts. If this is the case, you have no alternative but to take your investigation to the judge and let the judge see the truth. Remember judges are also attorneys, and generally they think logically and practically. Judges like good evidence because they are trained to weigh the evidence you produce. I have seen judges outraged by psychologists who testify in court. I have seen them all but accuse psychologists of quackery.

When you go to trial and you are prepared, the judge might award you custody even if that contradicts the psychologist's recommendation. The reason is because your psychologist may have testified in that judge's courtroom before and made mistakes about who should have custody. So while judges generally award custody based on the psychologist's recommendation, there are occasions when the evidence is so compelling they simply cannot accept the psychologist's evaluation.

You might be in court months or years after your trial because the psychologist made a mistake on their evaluation. Or the parenting plan decided in court didn't work for the parents or the child.

III COMMANDMENT
MANAGE YOUR CASE

Because nobody knows your case like you do, you must take an active role in helping prepare and manage the facts in your case. Most often, attorneys don't have the time and you may not have the money to have your attorney do every little thing on your case. So you must assist in preparing and locating witnesses and evidence in your case.

The best scenario is to win over the judge and the psychologist. This would mean the psychologist and the judge recognize the facts and evidence in your case. With both of these people on your side, you'll win unanimously.

Why Do People Lie?

Every day in courts across America people are sworn in before they testify. This means they are sworn before God to tell the truth. Nevertheless, people perjure themselves constantly.

In child custody, people lie in hopes of getting their children. Most people would, rationalizing it's justified because it is their children who are at stake (as though it is in the best interest of a child to lie in front of God in a courtroom). But what if you get caught?

A diary can help trap your spouse in a lie. One of the main purposes of the diary is to provide the psychologist with details about your life and your relationship. These details help the psychologist decide how your child will be raised and by whom. The diary may catch your spouse in lies, thus improving your position in a family custody study by the psychologist. Because the psychologist has such a big impact in your custody case, *never lie*! You may be caught and lose credibility. Yet people believe they need to lie about their spouse to win. That's nonsense. Yes, it's true not all psychologists will go the extra mile to learn the truth. Yes, it may be true your attorney may not go the extra mile to learn the truth. But once you get caught lying, unless your spouse gets caught in a lie also, you reduce your chances of winning.

IV COMMANDMENT
CREATE A DIARY

The diary helps develop a chronology of your life with your spouse. This helps identify the issues, personalities, witnesses, and evidence in your case. The diary should be a reference book for your attorney and psychologist in your case. The diary is the beginning of preparing your case. The diary can be painful and therapeutic but necessary to recall the events in your lives together.

Lying can and has reversed custody. Psychologists believe a parent who is willing to lie will teach their children to lie. This kind of manipulation is detrimental to raising children and it will cause more confrontations between the parents in the future.

Proving lies does not always entail a smoking gun, but it's a good start. You want to build as large of a fire as possible in your custody case. So the more you can prove—and I mean really *prove*—the better your chances of custody.

By using the investigative techniques described in this book, you'll be able to prove lies. It may take affidavits from witnesses who will attest to an episode or situation that conflicts with your spouse's account. It may take tape recordings. It may take police reports or other records. Whatever the situation, lies need to be proved. When you add the proof of lies to the rest of your case, it will change the dynamics of your case. The important thing is to methodically set out to prove your case.

There are going to be allegations by both parties as to who is the better parent. You are going to need to monitor the progress of your case on a day-to-day basis. Of course, I believe you need to investigate prior to your custody battle to prove the patterns of behavior I have discussed. Yet things change in custody cases daily. So you need to manage your case every day to combat the allegations and lies that will be perpetrated against you.

Is there overkill in child custody cases? There can be. If you are too aggressive, it can appear you are harassing your spouse. But collecting solid evidence about important issues is necessary. In my years working custody battles, I have used my opponent's neighbors and friends to witness conversations to catch them in lies. But again, lying in court is the biggest NO-NO!

One way attorneys uncover lies is through a **deposition**. The deposition or sworn testimony prior to going to court is very valuable. My beef about depositions is that most attorneys don't do their homework prior to taking one. Instead, they use the deposition as an information-gathering tool rather than an impeachment weapon. Simply put, if you investigate a person ahead of time, you can ask the right questions, thus catching the person in lies.

The attorney will have a printed paper copy of this deposition usually months before going to trial, which is something you should review closely so you can highlight anything suspicious and actively investigate it. If they are lies, they can then be pointed out in court. This is why you need to monitor and aggressively manage your case—the one who knows your case best is *you*!

People lie for the following reasons:

1. To improve their chances of winning custody

2. To protect themselves

3. To prove their case

4. To protect their child

5. Because they have alcohol or drug problems

6. To alienate the other parent from the child

7. Because they don't have enough money to pay an attorney

8. To hide an affair

9. To hide money or assets

10. To hide their sexual orientation

11. To hide their lifestyle

I've used the following tools to prove lies:

1. Interviewed and taped witnesses such as neighbors, family members, boyfriends, and girlfriends

2. Prepared a diary for the psychologists and attorney

3. Wrote questions for the attorney to ask the witnesses and the parent for deposition

4. Videotaped the parent driving without a driver's license, consuming alcohol, and so on

5. Gathered police, medical, employment, divorce, and financial records

What Do You Really Win in Custody?

After all the money you've spent on attorneys (not to mention the emotional cost), what do you have when it is all said and done? Maybe nothing! Custody is a word, not a possession and not a person. I believe women are more hung up on the term than men. If a mother doesn't have custody of her children, society thinks there is something wrong with her. Although there might be a stigma on women without custody, some mothers I have interviewed said they realized because of the ages of the children the father would be more suited as the primary parent.

When I meet women like this, I sense an intelligence and maturity a lot of parents don't have in custody cases. These women did not abandon their children. They did what they thought was in the best interests of their children. In one situation, the woman lived close to her ex-husband and children, giving her plenty of access to them. These people had a peaceful solution. Certainly this is an exception—not the rule. In this case, I would say it was a win for the family.

However, in extreme cases—even after one parent is awarded physical custody—the fighting rarely stops. The bottom line is that while both parents have the right to raise their child, some parents just possess more skills to do the job on a daily basis. If you're one of them, then the child will benefit from you pushing the case to the point of being awarded custody. However, even after you are awarded custody, damage to the children can still exist because the courts are going to allow the other parent visitation. And if that parent manipulates or brainwashes the child, damage can occur. Sometimes the only thing you can do to minimize the damage a child suffers is by raising them the best way you can and minimizing their exposure to the other parent. This is when the term *sole custody* has an impact, because when the child lives with the better parent the damage is minimized.

Often psychologists have told me damage to the child has to occur to actually change custody—meaning if you can prove the child is suffering, then the court will acknowledge your demand for the child. Personally, I have always had a problem with the court system being reactive instead of proactive. This is not always the case, but often psychologists will say they don't see evidence that proves the child is damaged. Well, the reason why is because the stable parent had enough influence over the child during the marriage that the child didn't suffer. But now there is a divorce and the parents are not going to live together any longer. Of course, that poses a problem because the child needs a primary residence.

Not all judges believe in being reactive in custody. Some believe in **preventive custody**. When there is a recent divorce, custody is extremely important and the better parent should be the primary parent. Each case is different and custody can be decided at any time after the divorce. This happens with fathers a lot. They don't fight for custody during the divorce and two years or more down the road they take their ex-wife to court because the mother plays games with visitation, has a new boyfriend who is abusive to the children, or she brainwashes the children into hating the father.

Winning custody can be a myth. If the bad parent gets enough visitation, the child may be impacted negatively. However, in cases of **supervised visitation**, a supervisor is appointed to watch the parent interact with the child so no damage occurs. This is rare, but it happens more and more today because of drugs and alcohol problems among parents.

The other myth of winning is if you have to file bankruptcy to finance your custody battle, what do you really have? I have seen custody cases cost $100,000. And I have seen them cost $2,500. If your opponent is formidable, you can count on an expensive battle. But the theme of this book is *evidence*. Evidence can keep your case from turning into the expensive custody battles you have heard about. It's generally less expensive to hire a private investigator than an attorney or a psychologist, but in some cases you'll have to hire all of them. But remember, if you have good evidence, the cost of a legal battle may be minimized because overwhelming evidence may settle the dispute before it even gets to trial.

Another consideration in custody cases is the battle itself. Custody battles bring out the best in people but also the worst. Mothers regard their children as possessions generally more than fathers. Assuming this is true, the perception of mothers in custody battles is the father would be trying to take their babies away from them. With this in mind, a fierce battle will ensue. The battle often will tell what tone the parents will have with each other for years to come.

The battle exposes strengths and weaknesses in parenting and personality because the battle often exposes some truths about the parents, which may actually benefit the children no matter what the outcome. The reason is that the parents may alter their lifestyles as a result (or, more accurately, the court may order them to change or alter their lifestyle by threatening to take the child away from one *or both* of the parents. So the battle may have its upside, but there are no guarantees.

You must make the system work for you. The battle, in my opinion, should be waged ruthlessly but legally. In extreme cases, it is necessary to be aggressive and clever to expose the other parent and their true problems.

Two of the problems I always have with my clients—no matter the case—is that they don't think tactically and they underestimate their spouse. So many times they have said, "They would never do that." And of course they do! But sometimes it is too late to document what happened. The element of surprise and being prepared are imperative in extreme cases or when you are dealing with a difficult personality. These are people who sit around all day just thinking of evil things to do to their spouse. When dealing with this kind of person, not only do you need to be aware and prepared, but you also need to think tactically for your safety.

Here are some questions to ask yourself when battling for custody:

1. Are you the best parent to raise the child?

2. Can you reach an amicable settlement out of court?

3. Do you have enough evidence to win?

4. How much damage emotionally will your child endure from suing for custody?

5. How much damage will your child endure if you *don't* sue for custody?

6. Will the other parent always be difficult?

7. Will your spouse change for the benefit of the child because you are suing for custody?

8. Can you afford to sue for custody?

These are just some of the considerations for fighting for custody. Sometimes compromise is the best solution. Be sure you consider all the angles before escalating the custody dispute.

Issues of Child Custody

Parents often misunderstand issues of child custody, which is, unfortunately one of the reasons parents make mistakes in custody disputes. Yet issues are the bottom line in custody. You must know and understand the issues before you can have any chance of winning. Furthermore, a good attorney can position your case to define the issues with the court. For example, the **lifestyle** of the parent is very important. Some judges and psychologists do not approve of a parent having a partner sleep over during a divorce, separation, or custody dispute.

This is an issue a skillful attorney can make relevant in a custody case because parents are supposed to be role models for their children, and this behavior sets a bad example. Furthermore, this kind of scenario can cause psychological damage to a child. It's wrong to place a partner into the role of a parental figure during a divorce because the child cannot adjust that quickly. In fact, some children never adjust to the broken home scenario. This is just one example of lifestyle being an issue. Others include alcohol abuse, drug abuse, criminal behavior, lying, domestic violence, and child abuse (mental and physical).

Some parents drink to excess in front of their child. Some parents use drugs in front of their child. Some parents steal in front of their child. Some parents teach their child to lie to the other parent. These are all issues that need to be addressed in custody. I have worked cases where parents make their children sleep outside in the cold or heat as punishment. So, **parenting skill** is a huge issue in custody.

Discipline is also an issue. Some parents have some psychologically dangerous ways of punishing their child. If this is the situation, your attorney must pursue these issues to improve your results. Parents manipulate their child to dislike the other parent. This is called **alienation**. They alienate the child from the other parent by degrading their ex-spouse, though it is hard to prove. Nevertheless, it is such a common tactic with parents that you must make an effort to prove it.

Another issue is **domestic violence**. If there are police reports regarding violence, you must use them in your custody battle. Violence has a serious effect on children in the home.

An issue that is very complex is **child behavior**. The behavior of the child must be documented. Some children are still wetting the bed at 12 years old. This is not normal. I once worked a case where a mother was showing scary horror movies to her child. These films traumatized this child and caused him to wet the bed. This is the kind of issue psychologists can identify. It's common sense to me, but some parents show their child violent or sexy films when they are too young to watch. It's a form of child abuse to expose a child to raunchy films.

School problems also are an issue. Whether it's absences or learning problems, school records are an important resource in custody cases.

Personality disorders are often cited in custody battles. Some parents have mental problems. These are often difficult to prove. This is another area a psychologist can identify, but they almost always need collateral evidence to identify mental problems. Collateral evidence may be police reports, witnesses, or medical records that may show mental difficulties.

Lying is a problem for parents and children. If the parent is a pathological liar, it could be evidence of a personality disorder. So proving a parent lies may lead the psychologist to the personality disorder. The same is true of a child. If the child lies to an extreme, it may be because the parent manipulates the child. Again, this points not only to the fact the parent may have a personality disorder, but the child may have one as well. There may be a cause-and-effect relationship.

Criminal activity is an issue. Typically, criminal behavior is an example of a personality disorder. For example, most thieves have a personality disorder.

Visitational interference is a common issue. A parent should not play "keep-away" with a child. If there is a reason a parent should not have regular visitation, it must be proved in court. Unfortunately, you've heard of parents disappearing with their child to keep the child from another parent. This is not the way to approach the problem of a bad parent. Prove, prove, and prove…you must *prove* the parent is sick.

These are many of the issues of custody. Naturally, some issues are bigger than others. It's the sum of the parts. The more issues you can put before the court that have merit, the better your chances are of winning custody. There's not always a knockout punch, so the more the better.

Visitation Exchange (Traps, Weapons, Tactics)

I remember when John[1] was returning his son one day. John was diligent about his visitations. Although the child was an infant, John religiously exercised his visitation according to the court order. John never married the mother of his son. His story is she tried to trap him into marriage by getting pregnant. But John felt responsible to the child and he knew he and the mother weren't compatible.

I believe the mother would like to have seen John rot in hell for not marrying her. She made it as tough on him as she knew how. Sometimes he would go to pick up the baby and the baby would not be there. According to the visitation schedule the child was to see his father within the guidelines the judge had written. But the mother did not abide by the court order. However, if John was five minutes late bringing back his son, the mother called the police on him for visitational interference. The double standard was enforced by the courts and the police.

Ironically, John had forced paternity on the mother by retaining an attorney and getting the blood test to prove it was his child and pay child support. Some fathers walk away from responsibility, but John not only wanted to be a part of his son's life, he also wanted custody. That day when John arrived to return his child, the mother could see

---

1. Name has been changed to protect privacy

John pulling up into the driveway. John got out of his car with the baby in his hands and the mother ran out and kicked John in the groin and proceeded to punch and kick John while he still had his son in his hands. The mother had already called 911 and reported she was assaulted.

The police arrived and began to handcuff John for assault. Even one of the neighbors lied to the police, stating she had witnessed John assault the mother. As the police officer was about to put John in the police car and arrest him John said to the officer, "Before you arrest me will you do one thing and listen to the tape recorder I have in my pocket?"

The officer listened to the recording and decided John did not assault anybody but quite the contrary. John was the one with the bloody nose, not the mother. And the officer filed assault charges against the mother. However, as you can see, the police use the double standard. They may be willing to arrest the male for assault but they only file charges when it is a female.

Visitation exchange can be a war zone. You never know what to expect. That's why I recommend you take a witness with you. This can eliminate the possibility of violence. If there is violence, you have a witness. I also recommend you take an unbiased party, such as a private investigator or an off-duty police officer. That way, if the police are called and normal procedures are not adhered to, you have an expert witness to evaluate them. On the other hand, an off-duty officer would know how to apprehend someone if there was a breach of the peace.

Awareness is an important aspect of visitation exchange. I have adopted awareness exercises I learned in weapons training to child custody. We used a color system of awareness. White is what most people are—unaware and unprepared. So your color system should be the following: yellow is aware and prepared, orange is preparing to fight, red is fighting. Of course you need not be fighting every time you are at visitation exchange. But awareness is important because you never know what you may be up against during an exchange.

John was prepared. I worked on his case and I instructed John to carry a hidden micro-cassette recorder in his pocket at all times during his custody battle. His visitation exchanges became part of his case. One reason was the mother denied him visitation, which violated a written court order. Another reason was the mother filed false police reports on John, which was proved later because the former babysitters were interviewed and they confessed to what crimes were perpetrated. The mother would set up John by not being home when he would return the baby.

John would go home waiting for a phone call from the mother. Instead the police would arrive and cite him for visitational interference. As you can see when you document these kinds of acts, the demons are exposed. This kind of ruthlessness can reverse custody if documented properly. I have actually videotaped setups of boyfriends picking fights with ex-husbands in front of children during exchanges. On the other hand, I have documented fathers getting out of hand by using abusive language or physically abusing the mother or children. These exchanges have become lessons in tactics and warfare.

In the movie *Bye Bye Love,* it shows fathers and mothers meeting at McDonald's on neutral ground for exchanges. This can minimize the confrontation during exchanges. But on the other hand it can hamper your ability to point or gather evidence in your case. If you want custody, you need to point out the personality of the mother or father. If traps are intentionally being set to show you are the villain, this needs to be pointed out by you. If you meet on neutral ground, it may not always be the cure. There may not be any neutral ground because the emotions are too high. But setting up the parent who sets you up is sometimes necessary to your case. Essentially, you fight fire with fire. Proving the parent is vindictive or confrontational can support your case in court later. Or it can help the court-appointed psychologist see what you go through just to exchange the children during visitation.

During exchanges you need to:

1. Tape audio and video

2. Take an unbiased witness with you

3. Be on time or even go early to scout possible conflict.

4. Keep a log or diary of the event

Your weapon is actually awareness to prevent a trap or setup. Other weapons are the recorder or documentation you acquire in your case during your investigation. The tactics are how you apply or use the weapons in your case.

How you apply the information you gather is important. When and how you use the information are vital. In the "Case Preparation and Case Management" section, I give examples of how to apply the evidence after you gather it.

Traps can exist in other scenarios as well. For example, often during a divorce or custody battle, a spouse may serve a parent a restraining order. It really isn't a restraining order but people tend to call it that. It doesn't restrain anything. It is really an Order of Protection Prohibiting Harassment. Often women will serve this on a man who allegedly is harassing them. I say *allegedly* because this document is abused often and judges know this. I generally don't recommend this document to my clients unless it is really necessary. I believe if you cry wolf too often, the judges resent it. So if you really don't need it, in the long run it can work against you.

People lie to judges saying their husband or wife threatened them or assaulted them so they can serve the document. The document might state the spouses shouldn't be within 500 feet of one another at any time to prevent a confrontation. If it's proved later the parent lied to the judge to obtain this court order, it will hamper the credibility of the parent later in the case. This document is used and abused as a tactic to keep the father or the mother away from their children. If this is proved, it again points to the credibility of the parent who is using this tactic.

There have been many times where I've seen one spouse lure the other over to the home to pick up belongings months after the Order of

Protection has been served. When the spouse knocks on the door, the police are called and the parent is arrested for violating the order. Again it is a double-edged sword. If the wife gets the husband arrested by luring him over, shame on him. If the wife is proved to be the instigator, shame on her. These are the games people play. This brings me to "The Case of the Murdered Fiancée."

The Case of the Murdered Fiancée

This case is most disturbing because it involved the most serious of circumstances: murder. This brings me back to my advice regarding awareness. We could play the "if" game all day long. Simply, this case reinforces my opinion that you can never underestimate your opponent. Because the murderers have never been arrested or convicted as I write this book, my analysis will mostly be opinion rather than fact. Nevertheless, I believe a lot can be learned from this case.

I took an interest in this case because I knew one of the people involved, though I didn't actually work on it. I've used court documents and newspaper reports to recreate it.

Jim[2] is the father of Tammy[3], a five-year old girl. Jim and his ex-wife, Jenny[4], had a joint custody arrangement, but Tammy lived with her mother the majority of the time. As in many divorces, Jim and Jenny didn't get along well. This was further compounded when Jenny's boyfriend, Butch[5], moved in with Jenny and Tammy.

Jenny, Jim, and Butch had one thing in common: They were horse people. They trained and competed with horses. Jim is small in stature but athletic. Several years older than Jim, Butch is the brawny rugged cowboy type.

Approximately two years before Jim sued for custody of Tammy, it was alleged Butch molested Tammy's teenage babysitter. This was a

---

2.   Name has been changed to protect privacy
3.   Name has been changed to protect privacy
4.   Name has been changed to protect privacy
5.   Name has been changed to protect privacy

good time for Jim to sue for custody. But for reasons unknown, Jim didn't. Even if the results were inconclusive, the allegation is serious enough for the court to review Jim's case. The police investigated the allegation, but Butch was never charged or arrested.

Jim had a tough time with Butch and Jenny regarding his visitation, and several times he was denied it altogether. This kind of tactic almost always puts a parent on an emotional roller coaster. The parent may have to drive for miles to pick up the child for visitation and the other parent may not even open the door. Yet the music might be playing in the home or the cars are there, but nobody answers the door. If the parent has a mobile phone they might call the police.

This scenario happens every day across the country and can have a catastrophic effect on the child and the denied parent. After a while, the parent gets so frustrated they might do something stupid. Unfortunately, their options are few. Most of the time your only recourse is to hire an attorney to enforce your visitation, and this costs money.

According to court documents, Butch owed tens of thousands of dollars in child support for his two sons from two different mothers, though the mothers did little to enforce payment. Court records also indicated over the years collectors had pursued Butch as well. I didn't find a criminal record on Butch locally, but my search was limited. I can tell you one thing, though: Butch was no Boy Scout.

In December 1994, I read in the newspaper that Jim's fiancée had been murdered in front of Jim's home. According to the newspaper accounts, Jim came home with his fiancée one afternoon and two people wearing black hoods were in his home as he entered. When Jim saw the intruders, he ran and yelled to his fiancée to run. Jim ran toward his neighbor's home as his fiancée ran back to the vehicle. She didn't make it. She was shot point-blank in the head.

Jim called 911 from his neighbor's home. Ironically, Jim had just come from his ex-wife's home to see his daughter. Jim had gone over there to exercise his visitation and took his fiancée with him. When they arrived at Jenny's home, there was a note on the door stating they weren't home. This was another example of Jim being denied visitation.

It was a 90-minute roundtrip ride to Jenny's home—plenty of time to set up the murder. Little did he know that when he went back to his house two murderers would be waiting.

According to the news accounts, there wasn't anything missing in his home. In fact Jim had even left a few hundred dollars sitting in a dish inside his home. The money wasn't taken. There was no forced entry. I spoke with Jim's brother a couple of weeks after the murder over a beer. His brother said Jim feared for his life and wouldn't go home. He was sleeping on the floor at a friend's house with a firearm.

Two years later Jim went to trial for custody of his daughter. Jim lost. Jenny married Butch. Ironically, in criminal law spouses are not legally required to testify against one another. One month after Jim lost custody he went to court again for contempt. Jenny was already denying Jim visitation again! This story is one that doesn't have a good ending. Actually some stories never end. I wonder if the judge felt he made a mistake when you consider Jim was back in court a month after he lost for contempt.

This is the abuse of power. This is why psychologists are recommending joint custody more often. They have taken the position if one parent has too much power they will abuse it. Jim must have felt humiliated. He spent a lot of money on a lawyer and a trial and he lost to his ex-wife decisively. And she rubbed it in his face a month later by denying him visitation.

According to court documents, Jenny's attorney alleged Jim was telling his daughter that her mother and stepfather had murdered his fiancée. If this was true, then Jim probably blew it in the eyes of the court-appointed psychologist. I'm sure the psychologist really resented a father telling his now seven-year-old child that her mother was a murderess. This is why controlling your emotions is so critical. The documents also alleged Jim taunted his daughter by telling her repeatedly she was going to live with him and go to a new school. This was a brilliant tactic by Jenny's attorney. The attorney, instead of trying to defend the allegation of murder, attempted to cut off Jim's visitation because of these allegations. Jenny's attorney was essentially accusing

Jim of being a fruitcake for telling his daughter that her mother was a murderess. On top of that, Jenny's attorney got a court-appointed child psychologist to evaluate the psychological trauma of Jim's actions. Again this was a good tactic.

This is a good example of when you need to hire an outside expert witness, even though ultimately the judge would appoint an expert witness such as a court-appointed psychologist to perform a family study to determine custody. Now Jim was in danger of two psychologists agreeing with Jenny's attorney. This would have been a knockout blow to Jim's chances of sole custody. On the other hand, even if the court-appointed psychologist recommended Jim for custody, Jim was still in danger of not winning. Most court-appointed psychologists are so-called experts in evaluating parents. But child psychology is an expertise in itself. So the child psychologist may still have more impact at trial.

According to the judge's order, he acknowledged Jim's fiancée was viciously murdered. He also acknowledged Jim had accused Butch of the murder and molesting the babysitter. The judge went on to state that at the time there was no evidence to prove any of these allegations, but stated if it were true, Tammy would be in danger. These allegations may have been a mistake on the part of Jim and his attorney. Instead of focusing on the merits of parenthood, it appears they focused on the murder. That's why I always tell my clients that you must put the parenting skills on trial. If they only focused on the crime, they were still falling short of the bottom line: who is the better parent or what is in the best interest of the child.

Jim still could show the issue of his visitation being denied. Plus, even if Butch was innocent of all crimes, he still wasn't Father of the Year. In fact, it could still be shown Jenny was difficult before Butch was in the picture. But she was even worse with him in the picture.

From my view, the judge was wrong to give sole custody to Jenny. Let's throw out the murder allegation for a minute and look at the merits of the case. Jenny had a history of visitational interference. Specifically, Jim should have logged and documented through witnesses that it happened often. Furthermore, Butch was heavy-handed or antagonistic with Jim. If both parents are equal, the judge should by law in many states award custody to the parent most likely to share the child or the parenting of the child. Jenny didn't share Tammy with Jim unless he hired a lawyer or called the police to enforce the court order. So the judge could have in all actuality awarded sole custody to Jim based on law instead of parenting.

This is why this case is so mind-boggling. It could be said the murder actually hurt Jim's chances of custody. Because of Jim's failure to control his emotions or personality traits, he caused trauma to his daughter, thus losing custody.

After reading the court transcripts, I was even more confused. The court-appointed psychologist testified Butch was evaluated with Jenny. In other words the psychologist interviewed them together. The psychologist said that when he asked Jenny a question, Butch continually answered for her. Finally it became confrontational. The psychologist said Butch tried to intimidate him. The psychologist told Butch he needed to take a secondary role in raising his stepdaughter. The testimony revealed Butch instructed Tammy to lie to the psychologist.

The psychologist also mentioned an episode when Butch watched Jenny through the window while he attempted to interview her alone. The psychologist said Butch tried to maintain eye contact with Jenny. On the stand, the psychologist also testified Butch lost his cool several times during his evaluation. Jim's attorney asked the psychologist if he read any of the affidavits he supplied. These were sworn statements of former neighbors and witnesses regarding Butch's behavior. The psychologist said he read them but did not call and talk to any of the witnesses. Jim's attorney referred to a situation several years ago when Butch threatened to kill some children with a gun who were living with him. The witness who provided a sworn statement lived next door and the children came over several times in the middle of the night fearing for their lives. The psychologist didn't recall this episode. Ironically the witness did show up to court and testified but Jenny's attorney insisted the information was too old to consider.

Jenny's attorney pounded out of the psychologist that Jim waited almost two years to respond with his allegation of Butch's molestation charges. The psychologist openly admitted he questioned Jim's judgment and that he made his custodial decision based on Jim's judgment of waiting so long to modify his custody arrangement. Jenny's attorney also affirmed Butch did well on his MMPI-2, the test taken by all parties. The psychologist said Butch did well on his and it didn't indicate Butch had a criminal mind. On the other hand, the psychologist said Jim's test showed he lacked insight into his own behavior. His test indicated only marginal validity. Marginal validity means Jim to some degree manipulated the test. He simply didn't tell the truth on enough questions and he was scored with marginal validity. Jim probably wasn't coached by his attorney on how to take the test. But it was obvious Jenny and Butch were coached for their test.

Most attorneys don't understand the MMPI-2, so they fail to prepare their clients for the test. Most attorneys and even domestic relations specialists tell their clients to just go take the test without warning them or preparing them. This is another failure of attorneys. Either they don't know any better or they don't take the time to prepare their clients. (For more on the MMPI-2, see "What Psychologists Look for in Parents.")

Because Jim's attorney failed to tell him what the test was like (or maybe Jim didn't take his advice), Jim basically failed the test. Jim's attorney also should have told Jim that psychologists rely on this test to determine custody. In my opinion the psychologist wasn't interested in the truth at all. He made his recommendation based on the MMPI-2 test rather than the facts. What I mean is the psychologist received a number of sworn statements from witnesses regarding Butch's past and his behavior. The psychologist didn't interview any of these people to determine the truth or custody. So the psychologist relied on his test because it's what he is trained to do. He's not a trained interrogator or a police detective. So his comfort zone is his MMPI-2 test. In addition, he is probably overworked and has a huge volume of cases. This means he won't go the extra mile for your case, though he should have in Jim's case because of a murder.

But in testimony in this case, the psychologist actually admitted researching the sworn statements is in some cases part of his job. Jim's lawyer should have rammed this down his throat. Jim's attorney could have impeached the psychologist in this instance. He could have attempted to dismiss the psychologist's evaluation because it was incomplete. I know I sound biased, but I believe Jim failed emotionally in this case. I also believe Jim's attorney failed him as well. They never brought to the psychologist's attention that Butch had two sons from different women, and that his sons each had the same name. They also failed to divulge that Butch never paid child support. If character is ever an issue, then this needed to be pointed out no matter how old the information is.

The sworn statements they provided to the psychologist had good intentions. But as you can see, he failed to consider them as evidence. So Jim's attorney should have hired a credible private investigator to interview these people and tape them. Then he could have insisted the psychologist speak with the investigator. The other option was to have the investigator actually testify at the trial regarding the sworn statements. Or have the witnesses testify themselves. They only had one credible witness testify and the information was stale. Jim's attorney again used poor judgment by having witnesses testify who didn't have credibility.

The issue that especially puzzled me in this case was that the psychologist never figured into the equation the loss of life. I don't mean the murder so much as the fact Jim lost his fiancée. The trauma Jim went through wasn't even mentioned or considered in this case. This case was hygienically evaluated. Neither of the psychologists wanted to address the nastiness of this case. They simply ignored the topics and relied only on their psychological training, which is pretty limited in a case of this diversity.

The child psychologist was court-appointed also. This child psychologist actually limited the visitation of Jim with his daughter. The child psychologist several months prior to the trial met with Tammy once a week. The psychologist, in my opinion, successfully drove a barrier between Jim and his daughter. Essentially the child psychologist spent a lot of her time asking Tammy about her parents. The child psychologist reduced the visitation based on Tammy's account that her dad spanked her when she didn't tell lies. Essentially Jim wanted custody but not until Tammy was ready for first grade. This had a bad appearance and Jenny's attorney brought this out in court.

Not only did Jim fail to go for custody when Butch was accused of molestation, but he didn't go for custody until Tammy was ready for first grade. Then he taunted her about it. So the child psychologist reduced his visitation. Because Jim only went for custody when Tammy was ready for first grade, it appeared he only wanted her conditionally. He would essentially have a babysitter for Tammy—a first grade teacher.

The other thing I thought was not only unfair but also dishonest and incomplete by the child psychologist was that she met with Tammy, Jenny, and Butch in these counseling sessions, but she never met with Jim and Tammy in these sessions. So she was making recommendations to the court without ever meeting Jim. This is baloney. This kind of analysis is a butch job—no pun intended. It would have been appropriate to have Jim get his story told as well. This put Tammy in a position of only pleasing her mother and the child psychologist should have known better.

The child psychologist admitted she made a mistake regarding the issue of Jim telling Tammy to lie. It was quite the contrary. Butch told Tammy to lie. But it took the child psychologist many visits to unravel this lie and a whole lot of money. In the meantime Jim's visits with his child were reduced because the knucklehead child psychologist couldn't figure this out. The fact is, although Jim had joint custody prior to his trial, Tammy spent more time with Jenny. This gave Butch more time to brainwash Tammy. So again Butch walked on water.

Ironically, during the 21 sessions the child psychologist had with Tammy (that's right, 21 prior to the trial), Tammy never said anything negative about her stepfather, Butch. Come to think of it neither of the psychologists did either. Tammy talked a little negative about her mother, and more than a little negative about her father. But nothing negative about her stepfather. I smell a rat. How does that happen? Butch gets her to lie to a child psychologist and she is caught. But before she is caught, her relationship with her father is affected because her visitation with her father is actually reduced. Now that she is caught why doesn't she talk negative about Butch? Fear! And it seems the fear is so contagious the psychologists feel it, too. According to court testimony by the child psychologist, the reason a child psychologist was appointed for Tammy was to help her heal from the murder. But during cross-examination the child psychologist said the subject was only discussed once.

While instructing Tammy to lie actually cost Jim his visitation, it cost Butch nothing. In cross-examination, Jenny's attorney got the psychologist to say there were no problems between Jim and Jenny prior to Tammy getting old enough to go to first grade. Furthermore, he said the conflict was because Jim wanted Tammy to live with him and attend another school near his home. That's more baloney. Jim had big problems with Jenny ever since Butch entered into the equation.

This case was a diatribe from the beginning. Jim just couldn't win. An incompetent child psychologist reduced his visitation. Butch had control over Jim's daughter. Butch was vindicated of child molestation. His parenting skills were barely challenged. The accusation of Butch killing Jim's fiancée was ignored. But experts were very willing to consider allegations that Jim taunted his daughter about changing schools. Jenny's parenting skills weren't even challenged. The psychologist questioned Jim's motives for going for custody. The psychologist ignored the sworn statements. The psychologist relied on a psychological test known to have a large margin of error. The psychologist ignored the emotional impact of the murder on Jim. The child psychologist ignored her mission of counseling Tammy regarding the murder. The child psychologist never met with Jim, violating all common sense and fair play. It was never proved that Jim told his daughter that her stepfather murdered his fiancée. On the other hand, I was right: Because Jim waited so long to sue for custody, it bit him in the rear.

V COMMANDMENT
INVESTIGATE YOUR CASE

Without investigation, you dramatically reduce your chances of winning. The facts and evidence in your case must be investigated to secure the truth about your spouse and their lifestyle. This means that most likely you will need an attorney, paralegal, or private investigator to actively go in the field to locate witnesses and information for your case.

Proving Child Abuse

Child abuse crosses all socioeconomic strata in society. Anyone or any parent can abuse children. There are at least two types of abuse:

- Physical
- Mental

Mental and physical abuse go hand in hand. It would take an expert to form an opinion as to how much psychological damage is caused by physical abuse. When a child is behaving abnormally or has physical bruises or abrasions, which are obviously not caused by playing in the park, it's time to take the child to a pediatrician to ensure the beating caused no real physical damage.

You also may want to take the child to a child psychologist to determine if any psychological damage has been inflicted on the child. The child psychologist can provide two solutions: The psychologist, through an interview with the child, can often determine which parent did what. Therefore, if necessary, the psychologist can report the parent to the authorities as well as propose a solution so the child can avoid further abuse.

When you take children to a pediatrician, make sure you take photographs of the injury as well. I will repeat this often: Everything you do must be **documented**. The information must be written down, taped, photographed, and put into a diary. Intimidation can have an effect on children. Some men or women rule through intimidation. And some parents do this to their children. They may yell, scream, and punch walls to intimidate their children.

Depending upon the severity of this parental behavior, this can be considered child abuse. If a parent punches holes in the walls, photograph it and determine who the witnesses are who can testify to this behavior.

Jeopardy or Imminent Danger

Jeopardy is a difficult situation to prove. I cover this term with kid gloves because jeopardy is difficult to explain. **Jeopardy** (sometimes called **imminent danger**) as a category can be abuse or neglect. However, I want to take it a step further in a quest for proof and evidence. If your ex-spouse brings a convicted child molester around your child, that's jeopardy. Essentially, they might be putting the child in jeopardy based on who they associate with. Some parents are foolish enough to believe child molesters can be rehabilitated. Whether it is voluntary or involuntary, the children are in grave danger around that person. Examples like these are almost infinite.

I worked a case when the mother was living with a convicted felon on parole who was a member of the Aryan Brotherhood. This guy was a gun-toting, drug-dealing, convicted felon. Unfortunately, his parole officer didn't care he was shacking up with a woman who had three children and that he brandished his gun in front of them.

This guy didn't have a car, so he depended on his girlfriend for transportation. Consequently, the children never got to school on time because they needed to be driven to a private school the father paid for. This is what raised the red flag. The parents had been divorced for three years. They told their father, "Mommy lives with a man who carries a gun." Once I found out who the man was I photocopied his notorious criminal record and obtained two affidavits from former friends who described his craziness and that drugs were consumed in front of the children. Then I gave this information to the attorney and my client—the father in this case. We then asked for an emergency hearing because the children were in "jeopardy." The purpose of the hearing was to change temporary custody. Based on the information, the judge awarded my client temporary custody.

This scenario happens every day in America, but if an attorney does not represent you and you don't do your homework, you won't prove your case. This is a prime example of what I am talking about. The parent puts the children at risk because of the people they "choose" to associate with. As my mother used to say, "You are the company you keep."

Parenting Skills: The Lost Art

Not only do I need to prove the other parent is unfit, I also need to prove my client is fit. Two wrongs do not make a right, and I have worked cases where the lesser of two evils became the custodial parent.

Some people are just plain crazy. Parenting skills must be put on trial. What stands before a child is a lifetime of happiness and achievement or heartache and fear. Leadership can make a huge difference in children. That's why you often see examples of children who are seemingly useless but they go in the armed forces for a couple of years and when they come out, they are squared away ladies and gentlemen. And the reason is no surprise to me—it's because of leadership. Children are waiting to be led—don't let them down.

I consulted on a case where the parents of a nude dancer wanted me to help their daughter in a custody case. She had a boy out of wedlock and she wanted me to prove a series of things. This was a twisted situation that involved kidnapping and guns being pulled on people. Of course, that was a concern of mine, but not for my safety. My concern was the type of people I was dealing with. At dinner at their rented home (they often moved), the dancer showed me a nude photograph of herself from an adult magazine. I didn't know if she was proud of it or if she wanted to expose (no pun intended) her weaknesses. After listening to their one-sided story, I told them in my opinion what they needed to do:

1. Take parenting classes.

2. Take weekly urine tests to prove no drug use.

3. Take a part-time day job, not in a club or restaurant or where alcohol is served.

4. Enroll in a vocational school that could train them for a specific job in a short period of time to earn income.

5. Live with their parents for moral and financial support.

6. Pray.

It was rather obvious the dancer's parents needed a dose of reality. I never heard from those people again. I guess they didn't take my advice. That's an example of working for the wrong animal. Putting these parenting skills on trial would be suicide.

Later in this book I'll go over tactics and evidence collection regarding the proof of bad parenting skills. But for now I want you to be thinking of issues that affect custody.

II

Attorneys

How to Choose a Lawyer

Picking a lawyer is critical to your case. Let's face it; some attorneys are better than others. Years ago in America when there weren't so many attorneys, we, the public, believed they were highly intelligent and even ethical. That's not the case today. The fact is there are a lot of knuckle-heads who are attorneys. And some of them are just common thieves. But the same dilemma continues every day in America when it comes to choosing an attorney. After all, they are a necessary evil. Personally, I have little use for most of them. But they have a huge impact on this country.

Picking an attorney who specializes is usually the best way to select an attorney in a given case. There are areas of specialization of law practice. The state bar (a membership of attorneys licensed to practice law in your state) publishes a list of lawyers who are either rated or have certification for specialization, such as criminal law.

Some attorneys who have extensive experience in criminal law are certified specialists. The qualifications may vary from state to state, but the bottom line is they have experience in that area. In domestic relations, attorneys have certification as well. Some states call this **family law**, which is really the opposite. They specialize in the breakup of the family.

The advantage of a certified domestic relation's attorney is that they are usually better. They know the judges and the psychologists because they work the racket. Again, they are a necessary evil. Just because they know the judges and psychologists doesn't mean one certain attorney is well liked or respected by his peers or constituents. In some cases—maybe because they know the parties—it can work against you. However, generally speaking, domestic relations or family attorneys know how the game is played—and yes, it *is* a game.

Another consideration is choosing a lawyer with whom you can communicate well. Some attorneys have no "bedside manner" and they actually turn off their clients. Remember, attorneys are seeing clients at their worst. The emotion is pouring out to the attorney to fix the problem. After 25 years of practicing law they have heard it all. And some of them don't want to hear it anymore. Personally, I have seen very few family law attorneys over 40 years of age who weren't burned out. That doesn't mean they are bad attorneys. But they don't have patience or the bedside manner to listen to their clients' emotions or pleas or cries. On the other hand, some attorneys are so burned out they are terrible listeners. If this is true, they will do bad work because communication is vital to your case. You must be able to communicate effectively with your attorney.

To keep your bill down and to maintain a good relationship with your attorney, stick to the facts and support them with statements from neighbors, teachers, police reports, and so on. An emotional cry to the attorney doesn't solve the problem.

Because change occurs every day in custody cases, I recommend faxing updates to your attorney as events unfold. Sometimes a parent may get a new job or the children need to go to the doctor for some ailment. If the event appears to be significant, fax the information to the attorney to put them on notice legally. This means if your attorney knows a specific event took place and doesn't react to the court on your behalf, he may be negligent. In a highly publicized Arizona case, an attorney failed to disclose his client's attempted suicide a week before a hearing. The attorney was fined $10,000. This is relevant because it points to the mental health of the parent. If the parent is suicidal, the children in that parent's care could be in harms way.

The Case of the Weasel Lawyer

Case studies remind me of algebra when I was in high school. If you plug in the values, you can see how the problem is solved. Case studies are reality, not some theory sanitized for your protection. The real life situations encompass the circumstances, cast of characters, location, and environment.

A friend referred a woman to me who was extremely frustrated. For two years Carol[1] had been separated from her husband, Ted[2]. In the meantime, she and Ted had shared or joint custody, which didn't work very well. Ted was 36 years old, six-foot-five, and had a bad temper. He was a dominant type who ruled with an iron fist. Carol was 29 and passive. He was a salesman for a high-tech company and had a good income, while Carol worked part time and went to school part time. Ted ruled Carol and their two girls through intimidation.

Several years earlier, Ted had gone through alcohol and drug rehabilitation, which was paid for by his employer. He was a control freak, which is why he wanted sole custody of the children. His ego couldn't deal with the fact his wife simply didn't want to be married to him anymore. His revenge would be to win sole custody. He lived with his sister and her husband in a large home with a big yard for the children to play. Carol lived in a two-bedroom apartment. She had no car while he drove a new four-wheel-drive truck.

Carol hired an attorney for $200 an hour for her divorce. She had borrowed $8,000 from her father and gave it to the attorney as a retainer. They had gone to a few hearings when she hired me. The hearings were about spousal maintenance. Ted had recently filed bankruptcy in spite of his large income, though he had a good job and few expenses. Sometimes men do this in an attempt to complicate the divorce and avoid spousal maintenance or child support.

---

1. Name has been changed to protect privacy
2. Name has been changed to protect privacy

My client was extremely frustrated. The trial was to begin in four months and she felt unsure of anything regarding her case. I asked her if there had been any depositions taken and she said there had not, although one had been scheduled for her husband. I also asked her if there was a court-appointed psychologist. I told her that typically the child custody cases I work on usually have a family study performed. The psychologist generally interviews the parents and the children and determines which parent should have sole custody or if there should be joint custody.

I knew Carol's attorney because I had worked some cases for his partner before. But her attorney had never hired me. This attorney was dressed to the nines. He had a superficial tan and a monster ego. When we met with him, Carol asked him if he thought she should hire me. She said, "I think my husband drinks excessively and drives the children around in his truck drunk."

The attorney said, "If you can afford Guy's fees, it would be a good idea to hire him."

Then it was my turn to speak. I said to the attorney, "If I can prove he does this on a regular basis, then we can show it's a lifestyle and not just an isolated incident." Essentially, he would be putting the children's lives in jeopardy with this kind of behavior. I then asked the attorney if there was a family study being performed and he said, "No, because my client can't afford to pay for one."

I said, "The father can pay for it." He said we would have to pay for half and the father would have to pay for the other half. He went on to say the cost for us would be at least $1,500 for the psychologist. Actually, this isn't necessarily true. Sometimes the father, because of his good financial situation, might have to pay for the whole evaluation. It's up to the judge's discretion.

I said, "So, when it goes to trial without a family study, it would be Carol's testimony versus Ted's."

The attorney said, "I believe Carol will convey she's a concerned mother. And I will coach her testimony before we go to trial."

I said, "Carol told me they have had some bad arguments in front of the children during visitation exchange."

The attorney said, "Ted is heavy-handed and violent and this will work against him in the trial."

After we left the attorney's office, I told my client she didn't have a strong case. I said, "There's no current evidence about Ted's alcohol problem. Your attorney is using the money problem as a means to be lazy on your case. I believe without an expert witness in your case, you're sunk." Further, I said, "At least an expert witness or psychologist can say who's most likely to share the children and who the better parent is. At this point, it's who can lie the best in court and Ted's the salesman."

My client said, "The attorney should know more than you what's best."

"I agree with you," I said. "That's why I'm concerned about the way he's handling your case." I suggested she call another attorney and get a second opinion. "You can also call a couple of my previous clients and not only get a recommendation about my talents, but they can tell you stories about their attorneys and why they won their cases," I said.

VI COMMANDMENT
GET A SECOND OPINION

Get a second opinion from another attorney regarding your case. Your child is the most important thing in your life and getting another opinion is paramount to protecting their future.

The verdict was in—Carol spoke with another attorney and he couldn't understand why there wasn't a family study performed. Carol also spoke with a former client of mine who had lost custody and won it back because of my evidence collection campaign. Carol went back to her first attorney and pleaded for him to ask the judge for a family study and told him it was my idea.

He said, "Guy hasn't practiced law for 25 years or even been to law school. You need to listen to me. I'm your attorney!"

What we had here was an attorney competing for control of his client. His ego was hurt because he had given bad advice. While he chewed up Carol's $8,000, he had done nothing on her case. The issue wasn't the family study. The issue for him was power, and he had lost it.

When attorneys, paralegals, psychologists, investigators, and clients can get together for a common goal, the children will benefit. Well, finally the attorney petitioned the court and the family study was ordered. Now we went to work. I got on my computer with my client and we created a diary for the psychologist. The purpose of the diary was simple. We needed to reveal Ted's personality and provide an interviewing tool for the psychologist. In Ted's case, he was violent and used profanity in front of the children in restaurants and other public places. Ted partied a lot and there's no way he could make it through rehabilitation. After researching even more, I proved Ted bought a convertible Mustang while he was in bankruptcy and he kept the car at his girlfriend's house.

I interviewed the wives of his friends and they told me Ted had a cocaine problem. They also said they were afraid of him because of his temper. In addition, they said they hoped it didn't go to court because Ted would seek revenge if they testified against him. I was fortunate enough to coax one of the wives who knew Ted's girlfriend to call and record a conversation for me. Apparently, Ted had not changed and was just as abusive with his girlfriend as he was with his wife and children. According to the recording, Ted broke into his girlfriend's home one night, drunk, and forced her to have sex while scaring the hell out of her.

Because the trial was near and heating up, Ted told his girlfriend (who was a nurse) if she testified in court or talked to the court-appointed psychologist, he would tell the nursing board she had a cocaine problem. We had this on tape as well. Now we were building a personality type on Ted. I interviewed the babysitter of the children and she told me of Ted's failures to pick up the children on time, of not bringing clean clothes or shoes for them, and the abusive profanity he used while drunk. And this was just during visitation exchanges.

Now it was time to call the girlfriend and actually reveal information while questioning her. I introduced myself and told her who I worked for. The conversation went like this:

"Are you still dating Ted?"

"Oh, sort of," she said.

"Well, has he abused you in any way?"

"Well, I can't talk to you about this, okay?"

"Just one more question," I said. "Is he still keeping his Mustang in your garage?"

She said, "Can I take your number and call you back about this?"

"Sure," I said, and gave her my number.

You see the purpose of this call was to reveal information, not to gather information. I had already sent my report and taped interviews to the psychologist. I wanted to intimidate Ted. He would think I had a lot more on him now.

Ted would assume that for me to know about the abuse and the Mustang, I would have had to have performed an intense investigation of his lifestyle. I was betting on it. In addition, I thought Ted would call Carol and threaten her. I put a recorder on her phone to tape the threats. Remember, during the past two years the parents had joint custody. Basically, the children had equal time with each parent.

Ironically, Ted's girlfriend took care of the children when he had them. He would play golf and go drinking with his friends and leave the children with his girlfriend to care for them. What is even more shocking and ironic is the psychologist recommended joint custody, even though he could see all the bickering between two people who couldn't get along. Ted had even failed a drug test, and the psychologist had my report and the diary. To make things worse, the psychologist never interviewed any of the witnesses except for Ted's girlfriend. Two weeks before the trial, I told my client we needed to subpoena all the witnesses including the girlfriend. The attorney didn't want to do this.

However, I enlisted the help of Carol's father who insisted to the attorney it was necessary.

I warned my client that her phone would ring sometime before the trial and it happened. Two days before the trial, Carol's attorney called and tried to convince her not to go to trial and settle for joint custody. I call this the "attorney shakedown." This is when you, the client, have spent enormous time and money and the attorney is too lazy or unprepared to go to trial and tries to convince you not to go to trial because you may lose.

I happened to be with Carol when her attorney called. After she got off the phone, she looked at me and said, "Guy, you are a genius. You were right."

I said, "Look how far you have come. Look how much money you and your father have spent to get the same thing you have now—joint custody. And it's a nightmare. What do you have to lose but a couple thousand dollars by going to trial?"

Carol said, "I'm going to trial and you were right about my attorney trying to sell me out."

The next day we met with Carol's attorney and Carol's father to go over the case before the trial. I didn't know it, but Carol's father was an attorney, too. When we met the attorney, he wouldn't shake hands or look me in the eye. He acted as if I wasn't there. Not until then did I realize the attorney hadn't read Carol's diary or my report. If I hadn't hand-delivered my report to the psychologist, he never would have seen it. I knew Carol and I were in this alone. Generally, you need the blessing of an attorney when an investigator submits a report, and the opposing side must have a copy as well. My client's own attorney didn't. One thing the attorney did do was subpoena the witnesses to trial. Unfortunately, Carol's father had to insist or it wouldn't have happened.

The "weasel lawyer" told Carol's father in front of me at the meeting that I wanted to turn this trial into a circus because I insisted on subpoenaing witnesses.

This case for him wasn't about winning. It was about power. The weasel had lost his power. I had won Carol's father over. I had lost any chance of working for the weasel lawyer or his partner, but I didn't care. I'm a hit man in my business. If you want the truth, you hire me. If you want your case managed, you hire me. If you want a motivator, you hire me. But don't hire me and then handcuff me, because it won't wash.

VII COMMANDMENT
THERE ARE NO GOOD LAWYERS, ONLY GOOD PERFORMANCES

Attorneys are people and they make mistakes. Your attorney could have a good reputation and have worked ten good cases in one month and still do poorly on your case. It could be your fault because you didn't communicate with your attorney. Or it could be because you have a personality conflict. Whatever the reason, you have to take responsibility and find an attorney with whom you are comfortable and who understands the issues in your case, every case is different with different personalities and different issues.

The attorney had not read the report I had delivered months earlier. As a result, the trial was the next day and he had no idea what the witnesses were going to say on the stand. Even worse, he didn't know what to ask our own witnesses because he wasn't prepared. If the attorney isn't prepared and we lose, Carol and her children have to deal with the lawyer's incompetence for many years of anguish and stress. After the trial, the lawyer will get in his Mercedes and go home to his nice plastic life.

I simply told the attorney our witnesses are credible and it was in my report. I wanted to slice and dice this narcissistic, unprepared, fee-pounding weasel. But because the trial was the next day, we had no choice but to use his sorry ass.

The next day we went to trial. I went because I could impeach our witnesses if they went south on us. In other words, if our witnesses got scared and didn't tell the truth, I had tapes of their interviews. This happens sometimes. People embellish or exaggerate when you inter-view them and when you go to trial they backpedal. This can really mess up your case. Because what's really the truth? Once the witness gives two versions of the truth, you lose all credibility. My very presence can keep them in line. I can take the stand or play the tapes.

Ted's girlfriend was subpoenaed and she appeared. I told Carol it wouldn't hurt to tell her we had her on tape discussing Ted's misgiv-ings. Some attorneys would call this witness tampering or intimidation, but unfortunately she was still dating Ted, the girlfriend beater. But let's look at it realistically. Ted's girlfriend was there as a hostile witness yet she was there to testify for us. She knew a lot. And if she told the truth about Ted, he would be exposed for the tyrant he really was. I simply told Carol to remind her to tell the truth.

Ironically, this case never really went to trial. Once Ted's attorney saw the witnesses who were ready to testify, plus Ted failing his urine analysis tests for drugs, the party was over. Ted's attorney told our wea-sel, "You can have custody. I don't want you assassinating my client's character in the courtroom."

This is even more ironic because the court-appointed psychologist recommended joint custody. Even after he knew Ted failed the drug test. He hadn't read my report, either. I could tell because when he came to trial he didn't understand why all the witnesses were there. Well, if the jerk had read my report and had done his job, he would have interviewed these people to learn the truth. Apparently, both Ted and Carol tested moderately on their psychological evaluation. There were no knockout punches from the testing. Because these "knuckle-head" psychologists depend on the Minnesota Multiphasic Personality Inventory-2 (MMPI-2) as their bible, he recommended joint custody. (We'll discuss this test in detail in Part 4)

Not only did Carol get sole custody, she also got a new car (not Ted's Mustang). Later that night, Carol's father bought my dinner. He looked me in the eye while he held his drink and said, "Guy, you are my hero."

The Retainer

Let's talk about money because it is a subject attorneys love. Attorneys will ask you to sign a fee agreement. Ethically, they have to have a fee agreement with their clients. As you can see from the agreement, the attorney is already representing himself. Hypothetically, it would make more sense if you had somebody represent you for the purpose of the agreement. Nevertheless, it is a necessary part of legal representation. I am not an attorney so I am not going to lecture you on fee agreements. However, I have hired attorneys before and I personally would never do business with one whose fee agreement was a non-refundable retainer. For example, if you hire an attorney who requires a $10,000 non-refundable retainer, and for some reason you don't like or approve of their work, you may lose your money.

I have seen people retain attorneys and give them their life savings with the hope they can get custody of their children. Then a month later they fire their attorney for non-performance or whatever the reason and they can't get their money back. Or they fire their attorney and the retainer is used up. Then they're stuck with no attorney *and* no money. So what's the answer? Poco a Poco, little by little you release the money for the attorney to use. For example, if your custody case total cost is $10,000 and you release $2,500 at a time, at least all your money is not sitting in an attorney's trust account waiting to be gobbled up by legal gymnastics. I recommend you deal with private investigators the same way. Retainers paid out in small increments make accountability easier to control.

What Is Good Legal Performance?

I don't want to sound like I am passing the buck, but you need to consult a legal expert on this subject to get the best answer. I sued an attorney in my lifetime and frankly finding an attorney with the courage to do it was difficult. I also found out that accountability for their performance is difficult to prove and it appears to be more gray than black and white. I believe there is great potential for attorneys to sue other attorneys as a business.

There is plenty of room for good attorneys because in my opinion there are so few of them. I have seen attorneys blame judges or their clients for their losses. Attorneys cannot admit guilt or responsibility because they could be sued. I have had attorneys tell me they represent themselves first and their client comes second or third. So as you can see, you are not their priority.

There are options when hiring a new attorney. For example, at your first meeting, take another attorney with you. The attorney may be a family friend but isn't a family attorney. After all if they were, you would probably hire them.

Nevertheless, the attorney you take with you may help you understand the process of custody and how attorneys work. Also, the attorney will be able to ask the right questions of the attorney that you may not know to ask. The reason is because this may be the first time you have ever had to hire an attorney for this kind of case.

Having another attorney present may make the family attorney uncomfortable—too bad. In child custody cases, the future of your child is at stake—so don't be passive. I have known attorneys when they meet their clients for the first time and they will tell them anything to get their business. In custody cases, you are in a highly emotional state and the attorney may tell you what you want to hear. By having another person with you for your first consultation, any attempt to slip you a con job or take advantage of you will be minimized.

On the other hand, some attorneys are too conservative about the speculation of a given outcome. That is why you need to provide them with as much information as you can to acquire the best representation. Each case is different with different circumstances. Often, attorneys work the last case like the next case. That's not good enough. Pick an attorney who can form a plan, form a strategy, and who can tell you your weaknesses and your strengths.

For the best results:

1. Hire a family law specialist.

2. Consult at least one other attorney on your case.

3. Pay small retainers.

4. Communicate often by fax, phone, or letter.

5. Supplement communication with evidence, documents, witnesses, records, and so on.

6. Be involved in the strategy of your case.

7. Don't depend on your attorney to win your case.

8. Educate yourself on the subject through people, articles, books, and so on.

If you know other people who have gone through a similar situation, get their story. Maybe you can avoid their mistakes. Nobody knows the case better than you do because you have lived it, but you must tactically and rationally plot your case within the rules. Your attorney is your mouthpiece in court, but you must supply them with the knowledge and weapons to win.

People don't plan to fail; they fail to plan. So stay on top of your attorney because they're working many cases to make a living. Update them, but don't harass them. They'll resent you and it becomes counterproductive.

The Attorney Shakedown

The attorney shakedown can probably be employed numerous ways. One way, as I mentioned earlier, is the **non-refundable retainer**. When you put all your eggs in one basket, you have limited options. You do not want to be totally dependent on your attorney for results. You must have options financially and tactically. If your money is tied up, so are you. If you have a lot of money, naturally you have legal options by replacing the attorney you aren't happy with. So, if for some reason you have a **non-refundable retainer**, then you are not limited to that attorney.

If you do seek another opinion, you need to bring them up to speed about your case by providing as much written and verbal information as you can. You will then need to go over your case play-by-play. By getting at least one other opinion, you avoid being shaken down by your present attorney in terms of strategy.

Some attorneys will work your case until you run out of money. They may tell you that if you go to trial, it will cost too much money. This may be true. If you are going through a divorce and custody, the attorney will know your finances. They'll know how much money you have left to litigate your case. This is good and bad because they may work your case just long enough to spend the available funds. On the other hand, they may know your financial limitations and seek a resolution in your case as well. However, you may be gambling with a compromise you and your children cannot live with. Essentially, the attorney may tell you that you can achieve sole custody and several months later right before you go to trial, they will tell you to compromise.

This is a shakedown. I have seen parents with temporary joint custody during the custody battle itself. This is when the judge will award joint custody to the parents prior to going to trial. Usually, the discovery of the case will require a family study, depositions, and other legal gymnastics that take several months and sometimes years. The joint custody arrangement becomes a test period to see how the family deals with the arrangement. If your joint custody arrangement doesn't work, then it probably won't work later either. So, if your attorney tries to get you to settle for joint custody, this can be a shakedown.

Sometimes the court-appointed psychologist will still recommend joint custody even when they can see the parents don't get along. But that doesn't mean the judge will agree. Neither does it mean the judge won't award one of the parent's physical custody. That's again when your independent evidence becomes critical to your case. The evidence may not convince a psychologist of your case, but it might convince a judge you need either physical custody or sole custody.

You need to decide whether you should go to trial and have your day in court, or compromise and settle out of court with the recommended arrangement. Remember physical custody means the parent who is awarded physical custody will be the primary parent raising the child. However, if the parent without physical custody has money or is combative, they can take issues of parenting to court on a regular basis.

This means even after your agreement is signed, sealed, and delivered and it is physical custody, it still limits the parenting agreement. So remember joint custody usually has a primary parent designated with physical custody. But that doesn't mean you have sole custody. Because without sole custody both parents still have equal power legally.

Financing the Battle

The battle of divorce and custody can cost thousands of dollars. You may need to pay attorneys, experts, and investigators to prove your case. You will need to be aware and prepared. Awareness is discerning you need to change custody or a divorce. The common practice I have seen in divorce is that when the divorce is erupting, one of the spouses will clean out the bank accounts thus preventing the other spouse from having the financial ability to fight.

This is where awareness is critical. When you know or sense a breakup is imminent, you must prepare financially. This can be accomplished many ways. One-way is to salami slice the bank accounts ahead of time, slowly taking small amounts of money out of the accounts so the other spouse doesn't get suspicious. This can be as little as $25 a week. But months later it's at least a little money to get an apartment or retain an attorney depending on the circumstances. This is why when you know things are deteriorating, you must act. Another way of raising money is to borrow it. This can be from relatives, banks, or mortgage companies.

You might need to cash in investments, retirement accounts, or bonds. Or, you may need to sell jewelry, cars, firearms, or anything unnecessary for life. The important thing is to be creative and look for ways to finance your battle.

The Letter-Writing Campaign

There are some things attorneys excel in, and letters are one of them. However, I would be remiss if I didn't at least throw in my opinion regarding the importance and purpose of letters. Note, however, that not all attorneys are good letter writers. But attorneys generally like writing letters because it's billable and it's easy money. For example, if an attorney is writing ten letters a day on various cases, they stand to bill at least $1,000 to $2,000 a day. Again, that's easy money for attorneys.

But what is really being accomplished? It's strategy! The letters help to accomplish a goal or make a statement. The parent might be requesting financial records. If the parent doesn't respond or cooperate, your attorney should write another letter. If there's still no cooperation, then your attorney should file a motion with the court. This accomplishes two things:

1. It puts the judge on notice that there is no cooperation.

2. The judge can force the parent to cooperate by sanctioning the parent in the form of a fine.

If a parent is not cooperating regarding anything, the judge might become biased toward the other parent. Letters regarding custody cases can be written almost anytime during the case—and often after the case has been decided. The reason is custody issues are ongoing in almost all cases because parents rarely agree on anything in today's divorce world.

On many of the cases I've consulted on, I recommended to the parent to request more time with the child. Often fathers want more time, yet sometimes their knuckleheaded attorney fails to request it. It's the principle of incrementalism. Often custody cases take a long time to settle, sometimes years. During that time, a parent may not have a sufficient amount of time with their child to maintain a strong bond. So, in my opinion, your attorney should request an evening here and there to achieve more time with their children. If the opposition tells you to pound dirt, at least it's on the record.

Essentially, force the other parent to expose their position regarding parenting time with your child. If you do this several times during the case, you then have your attorney send copies of the letters to the court-appointed psychologist informing him of your spouse's position. For example, one extra day a month with your child is not asking for too much. Naturally, if you are requesting four evenings extra a month, you might appear unrealistic to a judge or therapist. A lot of this is predicated on work schedules, vacations, and other variables. The point of writing these kinds of letters is to force the rat out of the hole. Some parents just don't want to share their parenting time.

I sat in a conference room with my client and his attorney discussing his case. My client's wife was an attorney as well, and she was having an affair with another woman. They had five children together. My client had what I call "sperm donor visitation" with his children. He saw them every other weekend. That's very little time with five children—particularly when the mother was a working attorney. So there was no valid reason he shouldn't have at least a little more time with five children.

Often parents don't realize when they have several children that it's difficult to give them equal parenting time, even when they are living with you. But when they are not living with you, it is even more limiting.

I asked my client's attorney why she had not requested more parenting time and she couldn't answer. Frankly, she just hadn't thought of it. It was shameful in my view. These children were traumatized by the divorce. In addition, their mother was seeing another woman. It took the attorney two months to request more parenting time for my client. The opposition didn't even respond to us. The timing was actually bad because we went to trial two months after the letter was sent.

Ironically, I did help my client get a better deal in this case. The mother who was a practicing attorney really thought she was above the law. In court she perjured herself by telling the judge she sold the family van without the father's consent for $12,000. I proved she sold it for $19,000. The judge fined the mother *and* attorney for lying, then fined the mother another $5,000 for perjury. The judge also referred the case to the state bar for ethics violations.

In effect, my asset search in this case actually helped my client with the outcome of his parenting time. Because the judge awarded my client more parenting time than the court-appointed psychologist recommended, we revealed how difficult the mother was and that she had lied. This led to a better outcome. Again, there are three ways to win custody: win over the judge, win over the psychologist—or win over both of them.

III

Building the Case

Diary

I make all my clients create a diary. The diary is really the beginning of your child custody case. It also is the end of your custody case. What happened in your marriage or your relationship may determine who the custodial parent will be. You're probably wondering how the hell can I say this and what does it mean? Often people who live together get so close to each other and they are not aware of their illnesses or weaknesses. They may fully realize they are not compatible but they have no idea why. Sometimes their personality problems may be considered by psychologists to be mental illness.

The fact that a parent is mentally ill may be enough to determine custody. If a parent is mentally ill, obviously they could have an adverse effect on the children and their development. The only problem is proving it. Anybody will tell you their spouse is crazy during a divorce or custody battle because emotions are at an all-time high. That's why I recommend to all my clients that they create a diary. Essentially, the diary is a chronology of your life and how your life crossed the path of your spouse. Include how you met and the time line or chronology of events that explain their personality. Except you're on the inside and you can't see the symptoms or identify the personality problems. But events that have taken place in the relationship may lead the psychologist to a diagnosis.

For example, if your spouse seems normal and then without provocation screams or has violent rages, this may be a borderline personality disorder or your spouse may have no guilt and may be a sociopath. Or, your spouse may be self-consumed and have no guilt and be both a sociopath and narcissistic. Either way, the diary may lead the psychologist who reviews your custody case to the true personality of your spouse. Personality disorder or mental illness can determine custody. Obviously, if a parent is mentally ill, they are going to cause some damage to the children whether they are the custodial parent or not. Obtaining custody will minimize the damage. Sure, it's expensive to hire an attorney and sue for custody. But you have to ask yourself what it will cost your children in the long term if an unstable person raises them.

What Does a Diary Do?

A diary does many things for your case. First, it can get you thinking about your case and the relationship between you and your spouse. Perhaps it will bring back memories of how you met and the circumstances surrounding the relationship. That in itself may be very important. On occasion I have worked for men who wanted custody but they thought they didn't have a chance because they never married the woman. The mother may have attempted to trap the man by getting pregnant.

I have seen this backfire because the father may be able to obtain custody. Psychologists resent this and this kind of tactic or trap. The fact a woman would be so selfish as to bring another life into the world under these circumstances is a red flag for a psychologist. He will immediately examine that pretext and question all the motives. The fact is more men are winning custody today than ever before, but it depends on where you live.

I did not write this book for men. I wrote it for parents and grandparents. I have worked for all parties. But generally I work for fathers and grandparents. The reason why is because the mother usually has custody, so the mother is often the enemy. If fathers generally had custody, I would be working for mothers instead.

Unfortunately, there is a huge amount of custody disputes today. The reason for this actually is not too difficult to discern. People today simply don't know or care what is right and wrong. Love is rare because people don't have the discipline to enter into a relationship with love. Many people don't have the discipline or the constitution to maintain the relationship. The lack of love and discipline rolls downhill. Their children inherit the burden of neglect and abuse.

I make my living proving these cases. I may not be a hero, but there are children sleeping safer and better today because of me. Of course, you may say any investigator can do what I do. Wrong. I have lived this in my own family and my perspective and dedication to protecting children and working for the best parent is tantamount to my work.

Another aspect of the diary is this: It is a tool for your attorney. Your attorney will want to know details about your marriage or your relationships and parenting skills. These details may be what wins custody for you. The diary will tell your attorney how you met—when, why, and where. It should give a synopsis of your lives together. The diary should explain any abuse or neglect your spouse has waged on the child. Alcohol or drug abuse should also be explained. Key events that explain your spouse's personality should be included. An example would be if your spouse held a gun to your head on Christmas—which should be in the diary. Extreme examples of behavior must be included in your diary. This kind of information is imperative to a psychologist. This is probably the most important aspect of your diary. It becomes an interviewing tool for the psychologist in a custody evaluation.

The example before of holding a gun to your head or examples of domestic violence or constant verbal abuse must be included in your diary. These examples paint a clearer picture to the psychologist of what your spouse is really like. Not only is the diary a weapon against your spouse, but it can be a truth serum as well. When the psychologist interviews your spouse with structured questions, they will know the psychologist is prepared and this may expose more of the truth.

The psychologist uses the diary only if you supply one. Even if you don't give it to the psychologist, your attorney has something to base their case on or evaluate the client's strengths and weaknesses.

How to Create a Diary

Your diary should include the following components and characteristics:

1. Table of contents
2. Double space the diary so it is easy to read
3. Build a chronology of events
4. List important facts
5. Identify the important cast of characters or witnesses
6. Supplement the diary during the litigation
7. Include police reports and any documentation or investigation

Table of Contents

The table of contents may include topics such as: alcohol or drug use, infidelity, child neglect or abuse, manipulation, verbal abuse, alienation, and so on.

Double Space and Chronology

The diary should be in chronological order, double-spaced, and easy to read. It should be written clearly and concisely. You may want to create a few diaries—one for your attorney, one for the psychologist, and one for me with more details.

List Important Facts and Witnesses

You should stick to the facts and important details as well as a list of witnesses who can help or hurt your case and why.

There's no magic to a diary. You simply explain without bias what events took place. The details, clothes, or colors may not be relevant to your story, but if you feel they are, include them. But stick to the facts.

Just like a play, you may want to include the cast of characters in your saga. You should list the characters and their traits. The important characters are people who are familiar with your family and their lifestyle. I am always amazed at how little married people know about each other. The relevant cast of characters should include teachers, babysitters, neighbors, friends, doctors, police, counselors, and co-workers.

As I said earlier, you need people who are familiar with your family and their lifestyle. The interaction of the parents with their children is important to your case. If you want custody or want to be the primary parent, your parenting skills are on trial. You need credible witnesses to prove your worth. Your children may be your best witnesses. But unbiased witnesses are important and should not be neglected. If you have neighbors or friends who have a strong and favorable opinion about you as a parent, you need them.

Lifestyle is another issue all together. Witnesses for an unsavory lifestyle may or may not be neighbors at all. Rather, sometimes the lifestyle is hidden from the neighbors. Often clients have said to me that they live in a no-fault divorce state so adultery isn't an issue. Well, maybe in a divorce it isn't, but in custody it is! The fact that adultery is involved may paint the picture the psychologist needs to complete a thorough family study. Promiscuity is not a status symbol among mental health professionals. It's not your best weapon to win custody, either. It's like throwing logs on a fire. We may not have a knockout punch to win custody, but let's make the fire as big as possible.

When you don't have a knockout punch that shows beyond a doubt the parent is unfit, you need to examine the details of the parent's behavior to prove your point. The diary in itself may not expose your spouse or their problems with absolute credibility. That's why any documentation you can supplement the psychologist with is essential to your case. When I prepare a report in a complicated case that has many players, I develop a character list—what I call the "cast of characters."

As I said earlier, this can be used as a supplement to your diary. I don't recommend that you overwhelm your attorney or psychologist with information. Frankly, it has been my experience that sometimes they won't take the time to read it. However, if it is critical to your case, don't omit the information.

The best diary my client ever prepared included a table of contents. The table was broken down into headings such as Infidelity, Drug Use, Alienation, Neglect, Manipulation, Verbal Abuse, and so on. The pages were numbered, and double spaced with large type. This diary was user friendly—precisely what you need from a diary.

Case Preparation and Case Management

When it comes to case preparation, you can never be too prepared. The elements of a case can be broken down into parts. For example, not all cases go to trial. Some cases settle because of what the psychologist recommends. However, other times the psychologist sits on the fence by simply recommending joint custody in a case where the parents just cannot get along or make group decisions on the child's life. This is when trial is either imminent or necessary.

The elements of the case are the lawyers, psychologist, judge, parents, and children, as well as the evidence or discovery in the case. **Discovery** is essentially the facts and the documents pertaining to the case that will and should be used at trial. This discovery includes financial information, medical or health records, school records, depositions, witness interviews, criminal records, phone records, police reports, and driving records. Now that you have all of this information, what do you do with it? This is the problem! Attorneys are busy working a lot of cases and few will take the time to prepare your case as the trial of the century.

Nobody knows your case like you do. That's why you manage your case. This encompasses many things. For example, you need to decide which witness you will need to interview or depose first. You have to decide a priority and list or what you will do first in your case. You will most likely need to be your own case manager. This ought to be an occupation in itself. Events change every day in custody cases. So you need to be flexible enough to change the way you are doing things, if necessary. Being a good case manager means you stay on top of your case at all times which means you need to communicate with your attorney or the attorney's staff of any new developments in your case through faxes, phone calls, letters or reports. For example, your opponent may manipulate the child or the visitation schedule or any number of things. If this happens, your attorney needs to know the outcome immediately. As part of your list of priorities in your case you need to prepare your attorney or investigator to prove your case. The strategy should be a plan to expose the truth. The strategy should be combination of legal maneuvering and investigation to expose your opponent and their weaknesses.

Your witnesses may be the most important aspects of your case. What these people say under oath may make or break your case. I have seen character witnesses for the mother come in and destroy their friend by testifying because they were unaware and unprepared to testify. Most people have not testified in a courtroom in front of a judge wearing a black robe. It can be nerve-wracking even when the truth is told, let alone all the people who lie in court. This comes back to preparation.

Who is going to prepare the witness for trial? In my example before, the witness was a woman testifying as a character witness for the mother. She took the stand and the attorney for the father did a masterful performance of destroying her. They discussed what I call the "Forgotten Parenting Skills," in which the attorney would cite scenarios already documented by witnesses and police reports against the mother. The attorney would ask the witness whether she considered these examples good parenting. If the witness said yes, she would lose all credibility. If she said, no, she would be essentially testifying against her friend.

Preparing the questions for the attorney to ask the witness at deposition or at trial is extremely important. When you examine your case, you must know and predict what the witness will say. You must antici-

pate the lies that will be told. And from these lies you must also anticipate questions from the lies to counter the lies.

For example, if a character witness is going to lie, you need to examine how well the character witness really knows the mother or father
they are testifying for and how much access they have had with the parent interacting with the child.

If the character witness talks about what a wonderful parent they are,
we need to ask, "What is it based on?" I remember an interview I had
with a character witness who talked about what a wonderful mother my
opponent was. "Oh, she has the children involved in so many activities,
like tennis and swimming and gymnastics." While I was interviewing
her I basically impeached or neutralized the witness because there are
24 hours in a day and this mother actually spent no time with her children. All of the activities were just babysitters so the mother could have
time for herself. Yes, activities are important for children. But parents
need to personally interact and read to their children. The more children you have, the less quality time you have with them. Children can
burn out when they're in too many activities and by the time they are
teenagers, they are not involved in any. Instead of playing sports, they
are on the streets picking up bad habits. Some parents simply do not
have the patience or the mentality to interact or bond with their children.

Evaluating the witnesses is important. Some witnesses will only be
able to testify the parents are never home, they have a lot of babysitters,
or they would leave their kids with people who are not responsible or
credible. I like to prepare questions in cases that revolve around the
parenting aspects of the parent. "Would you leave your children alone
with that parent for an extended period of time? Why or why not?" The
answer could be, "No, because they drink too much, don't discipline the
children, or are violent in front of the children."

I prepare a witness list by priority of importance with a brief sum-
mary of what they can testify about. Along with this, I give the attorney
a witness data sheet so they know where they work and live so they can
be subpoenaed for trial. In addition, I give the attorney a list of ques-

tions for the witnesses, skipping lines on the paper so it can easily be read in court. Because we are a nation of addicts, a lot of questions can be centered on drug, alcohol, and sex addiction. Other questions will be around children and the basics of childcare.

Unfortunately, some parents just don't get it. They don't know what is good for the children. In "The Case of the Prison Guard," I prepared the questions for an attorney on the mother. I was able to show through police records, motor vehicle records, eviction notices, and witnesses that the mother had lived at over nine addresses in less than two and a half years. This is hardly a stable environment for children.

I then made a board like a graphic artist to use in court so the attorney could point at all the addresses one by one while questioning the mother in court. The reasons for moving were almost as incriminating as the addresses themselves. The judge awarded my client, the father, sole custody. This is preparation. You need to know what is important to the case in its entirety. And you communicate that to your attorney who in turn can communicate it to the court. Again, the questions you ask must be centered on the attentiveness and the interaction of the parent with their children.

At the same time, lifestyle questions are also a large part of the case. If parents constantly fight or have parties or hire babysitters because they are never at home, that is obviously an issue. I will repeat myself throughout this book to emphasize the necessity of being prepared in every conceivable way. I can be an inspiration to my clients or I can be a pain in the butt. Because the topic of children and grandchildren is so emotional, people tend to focus on the pain and revenge because of all the selfishness and fighting. I have helped many people in my business by getting them counseling or finding them a good attorney. Consequently, I have taught them my business.

Evidence collection has many avenues in custody and it can link your case together. If you tape an interview, what was said was said! If the information is defamatory, it will hold up providing you take the witness to task by subpoenaing them to court. And, yes, hold the tape over their head to ensure they tell the truth in court. It's a dirty business, but children are at stake.

Next, I want to talk about how records come into play in trials. Mental health records may show a pattern of behavior the judge can use to make his or her decision in the custody trial. Yes, it is true the psychologist will testify and the judge often decides custody based on the so-called expert witness, but not in all cases.

Some of these psychologists rubber-stamp joint custody in the interest of fairness to the parents instead of the children. The psychologist should not be an advocate of the parents. Rather, they should be an advocate of children. When the psychologist rubber-stamps joint custody, trial is sometimes unavoidable because the parents are at odds. They may think they've spent this much money and have gotten nowhere, so why not go to trial and take their chances?

Aside from the family study, there are often evaluations or counseling that parents have participated in prior to their divorce or custody trial. This information can cut both ways. The information may suggest counseling hasn't improved the mental health of the parents. Or it may suggest the parent has improved immensely, they acknowledged they have a problem, and they have confronted and have solved it or made progress. This depends on which side you're on and whether you really want to use previous counseling as a weapon or tool. Essentially, the attorney can suggest the psychologist did an incomplete job. Therefore, joint custody would not be the solution if the psychologist performed in this case. From that point of view, the attorney can put on witnesses to testify who may destroy the psychologist's recommendation.

Police records, like any record, can be a double-edged sword. Police records can have many applications. For example, as I have said before, in one case the mother called the police on the father for not bringing the child back from visitation on time. She filed a false police report and she called long distance from Sun Valley, Idaho. We knew that by subpoenaing her long distance company. This is another record we used to prepare and prove our case.

If you examine the witness or the parent while they are on the stand with this line of questioning, you can assassinate their character and by doing so set the tone for the trial. Records can prove abortions, false police reports, mental illness, hidden assets, trips out of town, affairs, child abuse, neglect, alcohol abuse, visitational interference, criminal activity, sexual problems, poor school attendance, no driver's license, no health or car insurance.

Preparing your case begins with the following:

1. Performing an investigation

2. Creating a diary

3. Retaining a qualified attorney

4. Filing for custody

5. Appointing a psychologist

6. Preparing for the psychological evaluation

7. Deposing and interviewing witnesses

8. Preparing your witnesses for court

9. Disclosing your evidence

10. Trial

The case actually begins with an investigation, which has many parts. You probably wouldn't file for custody if there wasn't a problem with the present arrangement. So, you need to choose an investigator to do the discreet research first, like school records, medical records, police reports, and so on.

Some records can only be gathered by the parent because of privacy laws, so you'll need to gather those. This way the other parent is not aware you are actually intending to modify the custody arrangement. Once you have the records, you can proceed with locating witnesses and recording their statements.

The order of your investigation is important because a sneak attack is almost always the best way to proceed. This way the other parent isn't aware of your investigation. As I have said before, when the other parent is aware of your intentions, they may try to change their lifestyle or tamper with your witnesses.

Next, you need to create the diary. The diary can actually come first as long as you don't contact any of the potential witnesses to verify dates and times of occurrences. The diary helps you cut through and clarify the events that led up to your divorce or your need to modify the custody arrangement.

Again, remember the diary is something you will submit to the psychologist to aid in the evaluation. So simply write down the facts instead of your opinion. The diary will be an interviewing tool for the psychologist against the other parent.

Once you have your diary and investigation in place, you need to retain a good attorney and go forward with your case. Again, finding the right attorney is a mission in itself. To the attorney, the investigation and the diary help clarify your chances of winning custody. The attorney will file for custody based on your investigation. Filing for custody isn't just legalese. The attorney needs to include at least a portion of the investigation so your case has legs to stand on. You may not want to disclose all of the investigation because you want to sneak attack with some compelling evidence as the case rolls along.

Next, the judge will appoint a psychologist to evaluate the parents. It is true some psychologists are biased when it comes to gender. So you want your lawyer to pick a psychologist from a list who will give you a fair shake.

If you have an investigative report, ask your attorney to send it to the psychologist. Some psychologists resent parents for taking an active role in their custody case.

Because the psychologist makes the decision on the future of your child, you need to be prepared. You also need to understand that the psychologist will give you a test to determine your personality. Your attorney should help you prepare for this test.

As you proceed toward your trial, you need to line up your witnesses and prepare questions for your attorney to ask in deposition. The deposition is a sworn interview. You need to prepare your attorney for any deposition including the deposition of your ex-spouse. Only you know your case best. So you need to communicate with your attorney often to monitor the progress of the case. Ultimately, your attorney will have to disclose all the evidence you have collected to the judge and the other side before the trial. So make sure you have turned over every rock before you go to trial. That's why the investigation is so important to your case. Without a comprehensive investigation, your chances of winning custody diminish.

When you go to trial, there will be no jury. The judge awards custody based on your evidence and the psychological evaluation. That's why you must win over the court-appointed psychologist. They have a lot of power. The judge doesn't always decide custody based on what the psychologist recommends, but it's been my experience that they usually do.

Common Errors in Custody Cases

We'll now discuss some of the most common errors people make when battling for child custody.

Failing to Sneak Attack and Gather Evidence

You have given your attorney the power to make decisions. Ironically, however, these so-called commanders of your operation make many errors, which could absolutely destroy your chances of winning. Custody is not a perfect science and many things can go wrong. Many attorneys simply create paperwork without a chronology in mind. For example, your attorney may choose to depose your spouse first rather than a teacher or babysitter. This is important because the parent may lie and the babysitter, teacher, or neighbor will tell the truth. These potential witnesses will probably not know what questions you are going to ask.

I worked a custody case where the mother was having men spend the night when she had visitation during a separation. She had a white-collar job as a human resources person for a high-tech company. Her baby was 20 months old and the parents agreed to split the time with the child. However, because the mother wanted to party and have men over, she gave the child back to the father during her visitation. So the father ended up having the baby most of the time.

The mother wanted a divorce, but she wanted the father to pay for the attorney and settle for a joint custody arrangement with no custodial parent. In reality, the mother's ego was at play. She just didn't want the father to be the primary parent. Mothers are often concerned with what people will think of them if they don't have custody. So she wanted a 50/50 split with no real custodial parent.

The couple was separated for about six months when the father called me. At this point he had retained an attorney but had not filed for divorce. He was trying to find an agreement his wife could live with. He secretly wanted custody because his wife had an alcohol problem. He was concerned about having the child in her care for extended periods of time.

According to my client, he had done everything for the child since he was born. Because both parents worked, he would drop off the child at daycare every morning on his way to work. He changed the diapers, cooked his dinner, read to him, etc. He said his wife would often be half drunk when he got home from work. After they separated, she really didn't want the child. Because she lacked maternal skills, she would play with the child and then want to put him away like a toy. Instead of raising him, she would often hand him back to the father on the weekends so she could party or go out of town with a man.

My client called me because he was concerned about the drinking problem his wife had. I knew my client from college. He was a party animal himself. However, since the child was born he had cleaned up his act. He had lost 20 pounds from abstaining from alcohol. I met with the father and consulted with him regarding his wife's problems. He said she lied so much he didn't know what to believe. His child was often tired or sick after being in the mother's care. He just basically said, "I'm not in love with her anymore and I don't care what she does when she's not with the child, but I am real concerned about her behavior when she is with him."

I told him his concerns were very real and that in custody cases behavior is an issue when a parent is caring for the child. I said it is a double-edged sword and the courts do not like spying in custody disputes unless we can prove a lifestyle that's not in the best interest of the child. Otherwise you will look like a scorned spouse who just wants revenge or control. Luckily, my client's attorney had not sent any letters to his client's wife and my client had not announced his concerns. This gave us a serious edge in custody. Unfortunately, every day in custody cases attorneys televise their concerns and lose the advantage of a sneak attack.

This common error destroys my ability to do my job, which usually depends on being able to stealth my way through a case. I may need to take photographs or perform a trash audit to prove alcohol or drug abuse, or some other destructive lifestyle.

Ironically, the mother had told my client that she had gone to AA and wasn't drinking anymore. My client had the good sense to tape record his conversations and he kept a meticulous diary of all the events and visitations over the last several months. He was able to document numerous lies. But what he really needed was to prove her lifestyle to gain custody. The first thing I did was to tell my client he needed an attorney who specialized in domestic relations. Typically, a domestic relation's attorney has a better handle on what the important issues of child custody really are. That doesn't mean they are stellar attorneys, but generally they are better attorneys than those who don't specialize.

I happened to work for the best attorney around. How do I know this? Because after working in this field for many years I have either worked for or against every divorce attorney in town. We thought alike and he knew the value of investigation. He also knew that in custody cases you sneak attack and get all the facts ahead of time to position your case. So we all three met and discussed a strategy to document her lifestyle and decided we needed some surveillance of her home to determine how she was living.

To save my client money, I only performed surveillance when the mother had visitation (besides, my client might look like a control freak if we watched her 24 hours a day). We wanted to see if she was drinking and having men sleep over when she had the child. She was living in an apartment, which was somewhat of a problem. Because the apartment complex was so large, I would have to watch closely to see what vehicles the boyfriends were driving so I could run the license plate later to know their identities. My client was able to identify one guy as his wife's co-worker who was separated from his own wife.

One morning I photographed the boyfriend holding my client's son on the apartment patio while smoking a cigarette with the mother. I was able to document these sleepovers several times.

Later, the mother moved into a house, which actually helped our case for two reasons. First, we would be able to quickly identify the owner of every vehicle parked at the home. These owners would later be witnesses for my client. By taking their depositions, we would be able to ask questions about the mother's lifestyle, such as drinking and sleepovers.

We already had photographs and my report to go to court if necessary. Plus, these potential witnesses would not know we knew the answers to the questions our attorney or we would ask. Again, we would sneak attack.

People often lie in depositions, but savvy attorneys can usually extract some facts. Of course, our attorney could always take my deposition, if necessary.

The second reason for our advantage was because I could now grab her trash more easily, which helped my client's case immensely. I found beer and wine bottles as well as the draft of a love letter she was probably sending to one of her boyfriends. It turned out, in fact, she was having an affair with *two* guys—both co-workers who alternated nights! And, of course, the child was present for all of this immoral behavior!

My client's diary became important when the mother complained to the father that the child was sleeping in her bed because he was having nightmares. So we could try to make the case that strange men were sleeping in the same bed with both the mother and child. My client, naturally, was ready to explode. I referred him to the First Commandment of child custody: Control your emotions.

We went back to the attorney and he prepared the divorce papers, including my report and our demand for sole custody, although we held back before serving them. We wanted to wait until we had a little more evidence of lifestyle before we served her with the papers. Shortly after, the mother was arrested for driving under the influence of alcohol—a felony because this psycho woman had the child with her when she was arrested. We served her for emergency custody the day she was released from jail.

The mother retained an attorney and fired back at us saying my client beat her during their marriage and that's why she moved out of the home. She also said she had the child 50 percent of the time during their separation, which was a lie refuted by my client's daycare records, diary, and taped phone conversations. When our attorney informed her attorney that we wanted to depose the boyfriends, the case settled giving my client physical custody with supervised visitation for the next three months until she tested negative for drugs and alcohol.

I believe she settled for many reasons, one of which was that her boyfriends did not want to be deposed, especially the boyfriend who went back with his wife. We succeeded because we were able to retain the best attorney, sneak attack, control our emotions, and pressure the other side with embarrassing depositions.

Failing to Investigate or Take Depositions before the Psychologist's Evaluation

No two custody cases are exactly alike. It is not a perfect science, yet parents and attorneys fail because they are not communicating effectively or do not have a plan to win. Most cases are lost and won on evidence and what the court-appointed psychologist recommends to the court. So it only makes sense to do all of your evidence collection and discovery *before* the psychological evaluation is completed.

This concept sounds so simple, yet in most cases attorneys actually fail to prepare their cases before there is a psychological evaluation. In fact, most of the time attorneys depend on the psychologists to win their cases. In other words, the attorney is just hoping the psychologist will render a positive evaluation so they have a good result for their client. Unfortunately, this is a pipe dream. In my experience—and this includes interviewing numerous attorneys over the years—a psychologist can turn sideways on a parent at any time and destroy the client's chances of winning custody, or even destroy a decent parenting plan of visitation.

It's ironic and even hypocritical that attorneys readily admit that a psychologist can turn against a parent in custody evaluations but they often can't see the value of preparing their cases ahead of time. This happens because attorneys are working too many cases or they just simply don't manage their cases. In fact, I believe it's more serious than that. I believe most attorneys don't know how to work a custody case. After all, they aren't trained to gather evidence, they're trained to litigate.

This lack of knowledge can be catastrophic for the children being placed with the wrong parent. That's why I teach parents to keep a diary, tape calls, and get involved in their cases. Simply retaining an attorney who you hope will do everything for you is rarely enough to win custody.

VIII COMMANDMENT
EDUCATE YOURSELF ABOUT CUSTODY

Most people have never been through a custody battle so they usually no nothing about the issues of custody. You need to gather knowledge about custody, the issues, the process, the do's and the don'ts. This can be achieved by reading articles and books, and by talking to people who have been through this difficult experience.

I fielded a call from a developer whose business attorney referred him to me. He already had retained a domestic relation's attorney. He told me he had a three-month-old son he had fathered as a result of a relationship with a woman 15 years his junior. The relationship had fallen apart because he would not marry her. He said she put his name on the birth certificate, but she would not let him see his son. This trick is old and it is still used every day.

A woman dates a wealthy guy who gets her pregnant. She wants the child support, but keeps the child from the father. Then the situation escalates. The mother is upset because her plan failed, or maybe they just can't get along. Either way, the child suffers. In this case, the mother was very difficult. The father hired an attorney to get custody. The attorney filed an order to have a psychological evaluation. The evaluation hadn't yet begun. This was fortunate because now I could at least coach my client. The first thing I told him was to stall on the evaluation so we could gather any information possible on the mother before the psychologist could render a recommendation to the court.

I could not believe the attorney actually told my client he had a chance for custody of a three-month-old child. I thought it was rather obvious the attorney was just trying to make money on this case. I told the client no judge would award custody of a child who was still being breast-fed. I sent him to the best attorney I knew, who told him the same thing.

Unfortunately, this attorney was too busy to take his case and referred him to another attorney. I knew this attorney rather well—a nice guy, but not real aggressive. I told my client this attorney was capable of doing good work, but that we would definitely have to stay on him.

This new attorney did not want to depose the mother. I thought this was bad advice because my client was going to be evaluated soon by the court-appointed psychologist, and we had no background information on the mother. Also, the mother had served an Order of Protection Against Harassment on my client, accusing him of domestic violence. The order was riddled with lies about my client, but the attorney didn't want to fight this either—more bad advice. He said the order would expire in two months, so it wasn't worth pursuing. Naturally, I saw it quite differently. What if the mother renewed the Order of Protection when it expired? Either the attorney was lazy or he hadn't thought ahead.

We still needed to fight for several reasons. First, the order was a lie and it might prejudice the judge. If my client didn't fight it, the judge and the court-appointed psychologist might think my client was guilty of domestic violence. Second, a court hearing gave us the opportunity to cross examine the mother and catch her lying under oath. We could use the court transcript later to depose her and pigeonhole her into even more lies.

What the attorney hadn't seen was the investigation I had compiled on the mother. I was able to locate a criminal record in another state. She had been convicted of a felony for exploitation of an aged or disabled adult. She had also lied on her real estate application by stating she had never been arrested or convicted of a misdemeanor or felony. So, she had lied to the real estate department when she applied for her real estate license. I also located other Orders of Protection Against Harassment she had served on other men. I was establishing a pattern.

She had been previously married and had trapped another man by becoming pregnant. But this had backfired on her because she had a miscarriage. She divorced her husband because she found out he had a trust fund controlled by his parents and he himself had no money. She had served the Order of Protection Against Harassment on him, kicking him out of his home where they were living together. I also discovered that her ex-husband had a cocaine conviction and that her previous boyfriend had spent time in prison for drug dealing.

Although the mother was well dressed and attractive, she had a sordid past. I had court documentation to prove everything in my report. So, the mother was ripe for deposition. When we met with the attorney, I unloaded my report. After close inspection, the attorney agreed we needed to depose the mother and entrap her into lying. It worked like a charm. My client and I had prepared the questions of her lifestyle for the attorney and she lied up a storm.

At this point, the child was not yet five months old. The longer it took to meet with the court-appointed psychologist the better our chances became because the child was getting older. At some point the mother would start dating men again looking for another sucker. This was good because she would start weaning the child so she could initiate her sordid lifestyle once again.

I explained to the attorney and my client that we needed to go to court to ask for more visitation for my client. This was a double-edged sword for the mother: If she denied my client visitation, she would look like a mother playing keep-away with the child. Essentially, the judge and the psychologist would resent the mother for trying to deny my client visitation. On the other hand, if she allowed my client visitation, he would be able to bond more with the child, which would increase the father's chances of custody. So the strategy was to incrementally get more and more time with the child. Once we had a court order of regular visitation, we could use the order against her if she denied visitation. If necessary, my client could call the police if she caused any trouble for him when he went to her home to pick up the child.

The mother played right into our hands. She lied in her deposition about her criminal record. She denied my client visitation and she lied to the psychologist. In this situation we were able to accomplish four things:

1. We investigated the mother before the psychological evaluation.

2. We took the mother's deposition before the psychological evaluation.

3. We were able to begin the principle of incrementalism.

4. We went to court to fight the Order of Protection Against Harassment.

We investigated the mother ahead of everything, which gave us numerous lies we could prove. We investigated the mother before the deposition. Instead of using the deposition to learn something about the parent, we investigated the parent first so the deposition became a significant tool to win custody.

We took the mother's deposition before the psychological evaluation. This way, the attorney could send over to the psychologist the depositions riddled with lies and supplement the psychologist's report with my report that proved it.

We were able to begin our principle of incrementalism by demanding a court order of visitation. My client was able to get more time to bond with his son. If she denied the father visitation, it could be documented and the eyes of the court would be on her.

Finally, we went to court to fight the Order of Protection Against Harassment. As a result, we were able to catch the mother in more lies on cross-examination. We then ordered the court transcript from this court hearing and went to work to prove perjury. Once we proved perjury, we could then notify the court-appointed psychologist that this woman lied in the hearing. Ironically, she lied regarding issues she had discussed with the psychologist about visitation.

I make this sound easy, and in some cases it is. But every day in courts across the country, parents lie. If you don't do your homework, you will not prove it. When a parent fights for custody or visitation or goes through a divorce, they are unaware of all the land mines thrown in front of them. Most parents don't know how to deal with lies or manipulation of the facts.

Losing Your Cool—Especially over the Phone

Escalating on the phone at the other parent can have an impact on your case because the parent may be taping the call and trapping you into a conversation that may cause you to say something negative about them or your child. Naturally, because your emotions are at an all-time high during a divorce or custody dispute, you are in danger of making negative comments. This tape-recorded conversation may be used against you in court or the parent may play the tape to the court-appointed psychologist. The psychologist may make his recommendations regarding custody based on these tape-recorded conversations.

Often during custody disputes the parents are not living together so phone communication is necessary regarding visitation, school, medical issues, etc. Parents often set up the other parent on the phone by pushing their emotional buttons in an attempt to improve their case. This setup can cut both ways in custody disputes. For instance, the parent may say negative things to the other parent while their child is in the room. This is called **alienation**.

Alienating a child from the parent is a huge problem during divorce or custody disputes. The attorneys, psychologists, and judges know this. Fortunately, many judges have become more aware of this kind of tactic. When custody disputes turn nasty, the parents often try to win over the child or compete with the other parent for affection and power. If alienation is proved, it changes the whole complexion of the case. Not only do parents lose custody because of alienation, but it is also harmful to the child.

Children often suffer in custody disputes from **separation anxiety**, a type of stress in which they are separated from a parent during divorce or custody disputes.

Children go through a tremendous amount of stress during a divorce, and when parents fight over them in court, the situation becomes even more complicated for the child. Generally, the child wants to please both parents. When the parents compete for the child's love and affection, psychological damage to the child may result.

Bad-mouthing the parent to the child is a serious mistake in custody disputes. Again, if this is proved, it can destroy your chances of winning custody. Unfortunately, this classic mistake is all too common in custody battles. That's why you must control your emotions during this difficult time. On the other hand, I recommend taping your phone calls with the other parent. In some ways this sounds contradictory. But it really isn't because you need to document their behavior. You must put their parenting skills on trial. For example, if a parent is putting the child in jeopardy, it is a parenting issue.

Parenting issues are almost infinite. Some parents let their children drink alcohol, smoke, play in the street, or play near a pool with no fence. These are the kinds of issues that need to be documented to prove the parent makes bad choices.

Many parents do not understand important issues in custody. In one case, for example the mother did not understand that it's poor judgment to have strange men sleep over while her child was in her care. To me, this is a no-brainer. But because she lacked morals, she didn't understand the psychological effect this could have on her child. She just simply believed the father was jealous she had men in her life.

I have seen fathers put their child in jeopardy by letting them participate in action sports without the proper safety equipment. A father may expose his child to firearms or take him hunting when he is just too young to be involved in these kinds of activities. Often the only way to document these facts is by recording telephone calls. However, beware of taping your conversation on the phone or in person because in some states it is illegal.

The Case of the Prison Guard

I like this case because it is not a textbook case at all. The fact is with all of the family breakups today, there is simply no typical case any longer. The impact of this case is interesting from the point of view that the father I worked for was only the paternal father for two of the four children we were suing for custody over. Two of the children he adopted from his ex-wife. When I say "ex-wife," I mean he had been divorced for four years before suing for custody.

At the trial, the opposing lawyer used some hateful and downright evil tactics. He accused my client's new wife of pushing her husband into fighting for custody of the children because she biologically couldn't have children. I could see the judge didn't appreciate this kind of tactic. The ex-wife certainly had her weaknesses, such as trying to undermine the children's relationship with their father.

As a prison guard, Jethro[1] probably had his weaknesses as well. His ex-wife, Jenny[2], said he was exposed to the dirt of prisoners all day,

---

1. Name has been changed to protect privacy
2. Name has been changed to protect privacy

every day and that he brought some bad language and habits home. That might have been true, but Jethro was a disciplinarian and he was honest. His new wife seemed to have a common-sense and caring approach to all of this. I did not see her as the pushy wife who wanted to raise four children. Rather, Jethro was just sick and tired of all of the games Jenny played with him and the children. Enough was enough and he finally decided to sue for custody.

Jethro was fortunate because his sister's husband was financially secure and paid for the attorney and investigator. There was a family study by a court-appointed psychologist, who didn't have enough sense to come in out of the rain. She recommended two of the children go to Jenny and two go to Jethro. Most judges and psychologists I have worked with generally don't like to split up the children. This psychologist didn't interview one witness. Although I supplied her with a report of Jenny's lifestyle, she ignored it. My report was extensive. I interviewed former babysitters, former neighbors, and former employers, and I accumulated criminal records and eviction notices.

Jenny was one of the more unstable cases I have seen. She had moved at least nine times in two and a half years. She rarely got the children to school on time, and she had moved the children from school to school. Fortunately, they were intellectually gifted and did well in school considering their attendance record. We requested the records from the schools to show the tardiness and absences. Her attorney pointed out the children were doing well in school so these records had no bearing. Our attorney countered they would do even better if they had stability and discipline.

After interviewing the neighbors and babysitters as well as locating a criminal record on Jenny's former boyfriend, I thought this case would be a slam-dunk. To me, there was no way we could lose. Her former boyfriend, whom she had lived with for five months, was convicted of drug abuse and domestic violence. Even though she had left him, it showed bad judgment on her part to consort with this guy. Compounding the issue was the fact she had moved many times and rarely held down a job. She mostly hung out in bars and lived on welfare or government aid of some kind, or she mooched off friends or men to have a roof over her head.

But the psychologist's recommendation was a setback. That would mean Jethro would have to pay child support for two children on a prison guard's salary while having to acquire a large home to house the other two children. Still I believed he deserved to win, should win, and would win if we did everything we could to plug the weaknesses in our case.

To minimize expenses, I interviewed the witnesses and secretly tape recorded the interviews. This saved costs on court reporters for depositions, which could run more than $1,500. As an investigator, this is how I can maximize my effort. By interviewing the witnesses and getting them on tape early, they are less likely to turn on you. Often in these cases, the witnesses will talk your ear off, only to change their story when it goes to trial. My motto is: GET IT WHILE IT'S HOT! Lock in witnesses before they change their minds or before the other side tampers with them.

Before you go to trial, you have to provide your opposition with a list of your witnesses. Once this happens, the other side knows who your witnesses are and they may attempt to tamper with them. If you go to court, however, you have their taped interviews to play for the judge if necessary. In this particular case, I sat with my client and the attorney at the trial. This way I could dispute the witness's testimony during the trial, which proved to be necessary.

Furthermore, I put all of the addresses where Jenny had lived over the past two and a half years on a poster board to illustrate the unstable environment she had provided for the children. During the trial our attorney pointed at each address asking her on the stand when had she lived there and why had she moved.

Jenny was noticeably nervous. She was wearing a red velvet-looking dress, though I doubt she had worn a dress since her senior prom. It's always interesting to see how someone has been coached by their attorney to dress for court. But most judges realize it's a charade. The shoes may be scuffed or the hair is matted. It's just not convincing.

For some reason, Jenny had regularly told her children she was dying. Maybe it was for attention or perhaps control. This is traumatic for children. Foolishly, she even insisted on the stand she had some terminal disease or ailment, though she was unable to articulate the prognosis. Our attorney didn't have to make a fool of her because the judge did it for him. The judge then demanded conclusive medical records to support her claim of illness and said he would not rule on the case until the records were retrieved and brought to the court. The trial went on and our attorney continued to question her about her residences.

I detected these addresses by accessing motor vehicle records, police reports, and eviction notices. It was iron clad. She admitted her former boyfriend had a drug problem and that's why she moved. On another occasion she said she moved because she was going to buy a home and had a falling out with the owner. Of course, she was evicted because she had no job or credit to purchase a house. They lived like gypsies, moving from place to place. Even her own family wouldn't help her. I spoke with Jenny's sisters who told me she had had a falling out with her parents over money and her pathetic lifestyle. Her parents came to the trial because they hadn't seen their grandchildren in over a year. Jenny even denied the children visitation with their grandparents.

One month later, I received a call from Jethro and I could tell he was all smiles. He called to thank me because the judge had ruled in his favor. The judge awarded him sole custody of all four children and Jenny had to pay child support for all of them. Because Jenny was unable to hold a job, the judge was lenient on the support. But the bottom line was Jethro had all four children, who were essentially out of harm's way. Jenny still had visitation, but it was within the guidelines of state law and it was minimal.

What Is Parental Alienation?

Parental alienation is when one parent turns their child away from the other parent. I have found alienation to be very common. In the overwhelming majority of my cases this is an issue for the child, and should be an issue for the court. However, brainwashing a child to dislike the other parent is difficult to prove. And even when it is proved, court-appointed therapists often ignore it in custody cases.

In recent years the debate among professionals is whether or not parental alienation is a syndrome. Dr. Richard Gardner wrote the book on Parental Alienation Syndrome, also known as PAS. Ironically the American Psychology Board does not consider parental alienation a "syndrome," by definition. While the debate continues, the fact is parental alienation occurs often in divorce and custody cases and can cause long-term damage to the child.

Dr. Gardner's research and book has caused a firestorm in the custody arena. Attorneys representing fathers have used his research and book as a tool to win custody cases. Consequently, mothers have organized to attack and counter Dr. Gardner's book. I actually disagree with some of Dr. Gardner's claims, such as the child should reside with the parent who has the strongest bond. But what if the bond was ill conceived? If the parent is able to bond with the child better than the other parent through brainwashing, denial of contact, and bullying the other parent, this is alienation.

This is an example of the parent putting their needs before the child's. If the bond is fostered through manipulation and bribery, this is an unhealthy bond. And frankly, a twisted parent perpetrates this scheme to deny the other parent a loving relationship with their child. Alienation is more common with mothers than fathers. I have seen fathers alienate as well, but mothers generally get more time with the child, which makes it easier for mothers to alienate.

I have seen many examples of alienation. Often a parent will get the child involved in an activity so when the parent arrives for visitation, the child doesn't want to leave. Or the parent will enroll the child in baseball or piano lessons during the time the other parent has court-ordered visitation. Unfortunately, this is plotted intentionally much of the time to reduce the parent's time with the child. With this scheme, the visiting parent falls into a trap of denying the child the activity, and they become the "bad guy."

My spin on PAS is twofold. First, the parent perhaps brainwashes the child to hate the other parent, which is mental abuse. Second, the parent denies physical contact with the child from the other parent. Either way, emotional damage occurs. What infuriates me is the reluctance of mental health professionals to identify and acknowledge the obvious alienation. Dr. Gardner believes PAS is more than brainwashing and programming because the parent actually influences the child to participate in denigrating the alienated. According to Gardner, this influence occurs in eight ways:

1. The child denigrates the alienated parent with foul language and oppositional behavior.

2. The child offers weak and absurd reasons for their anger.

3. The child is sure of themselves and demonstrates only hate for the alienated parent.

4. The child exhorts that they alone came up with ideas of denigration.

5. The child supports and feels a need to protect the alienating parent.

6. The child does not demonstrate guilt over cruelty toward the alienated parent.

7. The child uses borrowed scenarios or vividly describes situations they could not have experienced.

8. Animosity is spread to also include the friends or extended family of the alienated parent.

In a case I consulted on, the court-appointed therapist actually recommended primary care of the child to the father. Ironically, the judge awarded primary care to the mother. It's rare that the judge would award custody contrary to the recommendation of the court-appointed expert, however it does happen in a small percentage of the custody cases.

This case was a tragedy because as time went on the child did not want to see his father at all. In fact, a new therapist was assigned to the case and approximately two years later the therapist recommended no time to the father. The therapist stated the contact was too traumatic to the child. In this case, alienation was a tactic that worked for the mother. Here we have a therapist who knows the alienation is so severe that no contact is better for the child. This case was most disturbing because the therapist knew the alienation was incrementally getting worse and made no effort to stop it!

In another case I consulted on, the father was the alienator. During the divorce, the mother actually moved to another state to be with her boyfriend. She would visit her child once a month, sometimes less.

This made it easy for the father to alienate the child from the mother. The father wanted me to videotape the visitation exchange to show the judge the child did not want to go with the mother. The child cried and would not get into the car with the mother. However, I told the father and his attorney this actually makes the mother's case for alienation. The court-appointed therapist was able to detect the alienation and recommended sole custody to the mother. Before trial it was disclosed by the mother's attorney that the mother gave the therapist

World Series tickets! The mother's attorney disclosed it for ethical reasons or maybe because the attorney thought it might backfire. The therapist had not yet made the recommendation prior to receiving the tickets. But the judge ignored the information and awarded sole custody to the mother and she moved two thousand miles away from the father with the child in hand.

The reason alienation is so common is because many parents today have no ability to self analyze. They have no insight into their behavior. They put their interest first. Many parents actually believe it's a good thing to target a parent for alienation. In their minds, that target parent is really unnecessary to the child's life. A lot of therapists ignore alienation and paint the divorce as a "bad divorce" because emotions are high. That's baloney; therapists just don't spend enough time with the child in custody evaluations to glean the truth. When therapists ignore the obvious and focus on the irrelevant, the child loses.

Alienation can be very hard to prove because sometimes the effects take months or even years to manifest. I have worked on divorce cases that have lasted five years. In these cases, alienation was almost always a factor. Generally, if a case lasts years, the parents obviously are not in agreement on anything. If the custody case is a post-divorce matter, it can be tricky to prove alienation. For example, if a father doesn't have joint custody, he generally cannot take the child to a child psychologist without the permission of the mother. And some therapists will ask the parent for their parenting agreement to determine if therapy is even an option. In these cases, it may come down to witnesses to determine the alienation. It might be a teacher or day care worker. You generally need unbiased witnesses to prove alienation. Obviously, family members are biased. Unfortunately, they are often the people with the most contact with your child. I wouldn't completely rule them out, but a piano teacher or tennis coach is much better.

You would need to interview the witnesses on the record. I have been successful by persuading the witness to meet with our attorney in front of a court reporter so the witness is under oath. I call this the

"Secret Deposition." It's secret because we don't inform the other party that we are questioning the witness.

Some judges don't like this tactic. But in extreme situations I highly recommend it. I was working for a father in a divorce and his wife was living with an ex-convict who had spent most of his adult life in prison. He was convicted of armed robbery, as well as sex crimes. My client's eight-year-old boy was living in this home. The ex-convict's wife was upset about the affair and I convinced her to meet with our attorney. Unfortunately, the attorney had a scheduling conflict so I took the deposition. Our attorney used the deposition and all the goodies she divulged, in addition to his criminal and prison record, and filed a motion for change of custody. The judge granted our request.

I impacted this case the first week I was hired. However, to prove alienation, it may take several depositions or interviews to prove your case. If you have the option of taking your child to a reputable child psychologist, I recommend it. It may take numerous visits for the therapist to earn the trust of your child. You may need to tape your conversations with your child.

Wiretapping and Vicarious Consent for Children

In one case I worked, the mother appealed the award of primary custody of the children to the father on the grounds that audiotapes of coarse telephone conversations between the mother and the children should not have been admitted. The court held that the father could give "vicarious consent' on behalf of the children when the tapes were made, and thus the tapes were not made in violation of wiretapping laws. Be sure to verify that your state recognizes vicarious consent.

I generally recommend you collect the evidence and then determine how you can use it. If the contents of the conversations are so vile they threaten the welfare or best interest of the child, it's probably legal. I have found a lot of attorneys are not informed about vicarious consent, so you may want to educate your attorney regarding this tool. And this tool may prove alienation as well.

IV

Psychologists

What Psychologists Look for in Parents

This is not the Gospel. The following is what I have found from working and consulting on hundreds of child custody cases. I have interviewed psychologists in reference to which parent is better and why. I have sat in front of psychologists and explained my investigative report in depth. Psychologists look for parenting skills. Except that poses a problem right away. Because what do psychologists consider good parenting skills? It varies, but generally they look for the basics of parenting: cleanliness, sleep, nutrition, school, etc. Unfortunately, there is an inordinate amount of parents who cannot accomplish even this. If we can get beyond this we can look at which parent the child considers the disciplinarian. But not all psychologists understand discipline.

Some psychologists are preoccupied with self-esteem, the new buzz word among primary school teachers today. Some of these institutions and psychologists are more concerned with self-esteem than they are with **Mazlow's Hierarchy of Needs** (food, water, shelter, physical). The truth is children feel more secure with the strong parent. Some psychologists think aggressive personalities are bad among parents as well as children. It would be interesting to investigate the children of psychologists and see how they are doing.

Good psychologists look for which parent is most likely to share the children with the other parent. An example would be: You have one parent who is aggressive and possessive and possibly bitter about the divorce. The other parent is easy-going, passive, or affable. The psychologist might award custody to the passive parent, based on the fact the parent isn't vindictive or manipulative with the children.

On the other hand, the aggressive parent might get custody because the passive parent doesn't want to fight. The spouse torments the other by not allowing the parent to see the child. Or, the aggressive parent brainwashes the child by telling their mother or father that they don't pay child support and they don't care about them. Sometimes the children don't figure out the lie until they are grown.

Sharing the responsibility of parenting is a consideration for custody. When a psychologist is court-appointed in a custody evaluation, there will be a series of tests given to the parents. One of the most popular tests psychologists rely heavily on is the **Minnesota Multiphasic Personality Inventory-2** (MMPI-2) to determine personality problems. This test contains nearly 600 true or false statements. Patterns of responses are scored for individuals' tendencies toward hypomania, schizophrenia, psychasthenia, paranomia, masculinity, psychopathic, deviation, hysteria, depression, and hypchondrasis. We won't get into all of these terms, but suffice it to say that the psychologist wants to know if you are mentally ill or mentally healthy. The most common problems I deal with in my custody cases are narcissism (lacking concern for another person) and sociopathy (anti-social and having no guilt or responsibility).

Some of the test's statements are difficult to answer. For example, do you ever have thoughts of killing someone? The key to this question is *ever*. Of course, you do or of course you have. Everybody does and if you say you don't, you are a "liar" according to the test. This test, from what I have been told, really measures truth, manipulation, and guilt.

I compare the MMPI-2 to magic. Psychologists will not share this test with the general public, just like magicians will not share the secrets to their tricks.

If the MMPI-2 determines how much you see your children, you're going to want to appear to be the perfect parent. That's the problem. If you are honest on this test, you might be afraid you will be considered dishonest or criminal. The way the questions are written infer guilt. But if you really answer them honestly, you will look human. While the other parent is lying to the psychologist, you are really telling the truth and you are termed "human." Thus, a parent might be considered a manipulator or a sick person because they appear too good, too perfect.

The purpose of determining your personality traits or types is that psychologists believe your personality type in the extreme (like narcissism and sociopathy) could be hazardous to your children. That's why going through a family study or psychological evaluation regarding custody is like walking on eggshells. On the one hand, if you have an aggressive personality, it can be a problem. However, if you are too passive, your children won't respect you as a disciplinarian. My problem with the family study is that it is incomplete. If the psychologist came to your home or talked with your neighbors or teachers, they might have a shot at a good evaluation. Of course, the safest determination for a psychologist is joint custody. It's easy and reduces the liability for the psychologists. Although joint custody can be a nightmare, some attorneys won't tell you this. If you cannot agree on issues now, you probably won't agree later. If you settle for joint custody, buyer beware. If both parents have equal power and cannot agree on issues, what was accomplished by joint custody?

I have seen parents spend $50,000 on attorney's fees just to settle on joint custody without a trial. CAUTION: A lot of attorneys depend on psychologists to win or lose your case. In other words, the psychologist decides the fate of your children. Sometimes attorneys agree to this before the evaluation or the family study is performed in an attempt to minimize the fighting among parents. I have several problems with this:

1. Attorneys should not make agreements with anyone without your written approval or agreement.

2. Sometimes this is an attempt by the attorney to minimize their risk and participation in the case. Some attorneys just don't have the stomach to deal with a nasty case. So they do what

they can to minimize their ulcer. Unfortunately, they don't have to live with the result like you and your children.

3.   Your circumstances are always changing in custody cases. Parents get new jobs, want to move, or they might shack up with an axe murderer. The future of your child cannot be gambled simply because the attorneys want a clean case. The fact is some cases are nasty and there's no way around it if you are going to do what is in the best interest of the children.

Another glitch not talked about in the family study by your attorney is your divorce. Everyone gets focused on the custody issue and forgets about the divorce—except the psychologist. In fact, it's a big issue with them. The psychologist will want to know how well emotionally you are dealing with your divorce. They'll want to know if your children's well-being comes first or if you are consumed emotionally by the break-up and need counseling. It's been my experience that 90 percent of the judges award custody based on what the psychologist recommends.

Why do you want custody? The truth is a lot of custody battles are waged because of spite or revenge. The parent may say they want custody because they want what is best for the children, they want a relationship with their children, or because they are the better parent. The mother will say she can provide a more nurturing environment. The father will say he can provide discipline and financial stability.

The reason you should battle for custody should be because you are the better parent. You can provide security, discipline, and a regimen of nutrition, exercise, leadership, and interaction with your child. Thus you are creating a positive environment. From the negative side, you are rescuing your children from a manipulative, evil, incompetent, neglectful parent who doesn't know what is in the best interest of the children.

Things I Found in Family Studies

Most relationships or marriages have a passive and an aggressive (or proactive) personality. Sometimes the female dominates and sometimes it's the male. Usually, you do not see two aggressive personalities in a marriage. The fireworks would be everywhere.

Some psychologists are overworked and even forget which cases they are working. I have seen psychologists mix up their cases while testifying. I have seen psychologists change their minds on which parent they recommend for sole custody.

This poses a problem. On the one hand it might be the best thing for the children. Maybe after further analysis and investigation, the psychologist decides the other parent is the best choice. The only problem is the psychologist may appear to be unstable, incompetent, weak, two-faced, or bribed.

On one case I worked, the attorney was holding back a child molestation report filed by the mother regarding her roommate molesting her own child. I was working for the father in this case. This was the second time an allegation had been made of one of her children being molested while in her care.

The attorney said, "I don't want to sand the psychologist by alerting her about the report. I want her to make her analysis independent from our evidence." Apparently, this inexperienced lawyer believed the system works. I'm here to tell you the system works only when you make it work. The report or evidence stands alone. If the information is credible, there is no sanding. This is war, and war is won through intelligence and spying. If you don't expose or attack the weaknesses, you're not going to win.

In some cases, evidence is the only thing that will save your children from a tragic life. You need to be bold enough to do the right thing. Here are some of the "Do's" and "Don'ts" regarding children.

Do:

1. Follow the basics of child care.

2. Give the children positive reinforcement.

3. Share the children's lives with the whole family, grandparents, etc.

4. Discipline the children and teach them a work ethic.

5. Spend quality time with all the children.

6. Be a leader—set the example.

7. Say positive things to your children about the other parent.

Don't:

1. Brainwash your children.

2. Manipulate your children to spite your spouse.

3. Lie to your children.

4. Play keep-away with the children.

5. Beat your children or discipline them unconventionally.

6. Neglect your children.

7. Jeopardize your children's lives.

Let's face it, some people are evil and difficult. It's tough enough for your children in a divorce, compounded by the problem of you and your spouse sharing the parenting role. Through all of that, you also need to sort out the finances and still get along. Don't hold your breath.

Sometimes the MMPI-2 fails to expose a personality problem. Women are much better at camouflage and concealment than men. Women are detail specialists and emotion sometimes turns into Academy Award performances in court as well as in front of the psychologist. Men, on the other hand, tend to be confrontational, be open, or show their frustration and temperament. Depending on the psychologist, this can work against them if a father is open and honest about his feelings toward his wife during a custody evaluation.

The father will most likely admit he's bitter, frustrated, and mad as hell. This could really work against him because the wife may be a hell of a manipulator. She may appear to be poised, rational, or well adjusted to the emotional aspects of the divorce and play a game with the psychologist to the point she goes undetected. In the end, this father may suffer through years of torment. The mother may use the children as a weapon against her husband. She may really be the one who is cold or evil but she hides her personality and agenda from the psychologist.

By the same token, the father may be a salesman and try to out-point the mother. If your lawyer depends on the psychologist to win your case or figure out your spouse, good luck! Sometimes, the only way to prove what kind of personality type a given subject has is through evidence collection. Without evidence, you and your children may become statistics.

One more note about psychologists—they are overworked, forgetful, arrogant, and *human*. Are you sure you want to depend on the court-appointed psychologist to win and expose your spouse's problems?

Overcoming the Evaluation

If you answered the questions on the MMPI-2, you may be out of the woods regarding your evaluation. Maybe you answered the questions truthfully and you rewarded yourself with a good score. I have seen parents do rather well on their psychological tests and still get shafted on their custody arrangements. I have seen parents do poorly on psychological tests and still do well on their custody arrangements. What I mean by "arrangement" is the parent may not have sole custody but they still may have 50-percent custody of their child. For a father, this can be a good arrangement in terms of time spent with his child. A mother may not like this arrangement because she believes she is a better parent than the father.

Most attorneys will agree that generally mothers have an advantage in the court system. When mothers don't receive this advantage, society often thinks there is something wrong with them. This isn't necessarily true. Some judges and psychologists bend over backward to be fair. But many parents come out of a psychological evaluation feeling frustrated and betrayed for many reasons. Sometimes the parent will upset the psychologist by trying to do his job for him. This is a bad idea. You don't try to tell a pilot how to fly a plane! Don't try to tell a Ph.D. how to do their job.

Often, a parent will try to describe their spouse by using labels or psychological terms. This is another bad idea. Psychologists resent this. Let them use their terms to describe traits and personality disorders. You need to appear human, so you need to admit to shortcomings. If you boast you are always right and your spouse is always wrong, most likely the psychologist will resent you.

It is true psychologists get fooled every day in psychological evaluations. After all, psychology is not a perfect science. I find it difficult to believe a psychologist can give a parent a test and a few interviews and do an adequate job. That's why throughout this book I refer to evidence constantly to prove your case. This evidence needs to be in front of the psychologist. And it is your attorney's responsibility to provide the psychologist with as much compelling evidence as they can to prove your case. Often, I find that attorneys work their cases backward. They do their discovery and evidence collection *after* the psychologist has already completed his psychological evaluation. The problem with this is if the evaluation is not favorable to the client, they are going to have trouble digging the client out of a hole. So, their discovery or evidence is too late to impact their case.

Generally, it is more advantageous to collect the evidence *before* the psychologist does the evaluation. This gives you the opportunity to point out parenting problems, personality problems, lies, behavior problems, violence, crimes, alcohol or drug abuse, alienation, brainwashing, visitation problems, and any other issues the psychologist doesn't have the time or ability to examine.

Typically, custody disputes begin with a divorce. During a divorce the court will generally order a temporary living and visitation arrangement. During this period, events may happen on a daily basis. You may have problems with your spouse regarding visitation, or they may begin dating an abusive person. If this is true, it can have a serious impact on the child and the child's behavior. So, if your psychological evaluation is completed before this change in circumstances, you may lose the opportunity to use this new evidence in your case. I believe it is generally better to move slowly with the psychological evaluation because you may be able to use and gather evidence as it rears its ugly head during your separation.

I have worked on cases where the psychologist completed his evaluation, but it became outdated because too many circumstances changed or events took place that changed the dynamics of the case. For example, the psychologist may determine that the mother be awarded sole custody. In this case, the father would get visitation with his child every other weekend. This arrangement would only give the father eight days per month with his child, or 25 percent for the father and 75 percent for the mother.

Maybe this arrangement is fine if the child is in school because parents usually work. When children are in school, parents and children don't have that much time together anyway because all parties are busy. However, if the child is an infant, more time might be needed to bond. If the father only gets eight days a month with his child, can they sufficiently bond?

Many psychologists I have interviewed say the father needs more time with the child at a young age to bond. Yet I have seen in many cases like this where the psychologist recommends to the court this kind of an arrangement anyway. The psychologist may defend their recommendation based on psychological testing of the parents. Or they may state it's a high-conflict case and the parents cannot get along. They may ignore some issues and capitalize on other issues. They might even be biased toward fathers or mothers, giving one parent the advantage even before the evaluation begins.

Just as there are biased psychologists, there are also dishonest and incompetent ones. Some are burned out and some get fooled by clever parents. Of course, not all psychologists fit these descriptions. Some are fair and very competent. But if you have a psychologist who is unfair or incompetent, your relationship with your child is in jeopardy. A bad evaluation can cause many problems for you and your child for many years. The courts value the psychologist's evaluation. Many of these court-appointed psychologists enjoy outstanding reputations, so the courts rely on the psychologist's evaluation.

While the evaluation can be overcome, it is a painstaking task. I have worked on many cases where the evaluation wasn't favorable for my clients and we were still able to impact the judge and improve the arrangement. Custody is just a word. If my client receives a bad evaluation and we are able to get them a better deal, I believe I have done my job. If my clients are able to gain more time with their child even when the psychologist has recommended less time, we have succeeded.

While it's possible to win sole custody even when the psychologist has recommended sole custody to the other parent, it's rare, because—again—the courts rely on the psychologists as experts to determine the living arrangement, giving the psychologists instant credibility with the judges. On the other hand, the parents have to prove themselves in court if they are going to overcome the psychological evaluation. Many attorneys will not attack the credibility of a psychologist.

When you choose an attorney, you need to ask him whether he's willing to be aggressive with the psychologist if you receive an unfavorable evaluation. I have worked with many domestic relations attorneys who don't understand psychology, personality disorders, or psychological testing. This poses a serious problem for the client because without an understanding of the subject, it's difficult for an attorney to cross-examine a psychologist.

If you receive an unfavorable evaluation, you may need to:

1. Investigate any facts of your case the psychologist failed to consider or failed to investigate.

2. Hire another psychologist or expert to critique the unfavorable evaluation.

3. Subpoena the psychologist's test results and notes.

4. Take the deposition of a psychologist.

If a psychologist failed to interview or gather collateral information in your case, you may be able to overcome his evaluation. In other words, you need to be able to attack the evaluation because it is incomplete or there is new evidence that changes the outcome.

For example, I worked a case where the psychologist told both parents during the evaluation not to date or start any new relationships because it would confuse a three-year-old. The psychologist simply stated that a new boyfriend or girlfriend was a "no-no" because the child would be confused enough from the separation. The psychologist said it was in the child's best interest not to be exposed to a new mother or father figure until the divorce was complete. Even then the psychologist said the partners should be in a permanent relationship, not just casual sleepovers in front of the child. In this particular case, the mother did just what the psychologist warned her not to do. The mother started a new relationship with a man who spent an enormous amount of time at the home, including sleepovers while the child was present.

The only problem was the psychologist had already awarded the mother 75 percent of the time with the child as the final recommendation to the court. Plus, the psychologist noted many events and discrepancies in the report that were not true. The psychologist interviewed 11 witnesses for the mother and only three for the father. The witnesses for the mother were mostly family members. (I don't have to tell you how biased family members can be in a heated divorce and custody dispute.) The interviews are what I refer to as **collateral information**. Collateral information is just information gathered outside of the psychological testing.

I refer to collateral information as evidence, which in many cases can change the outcome of an evaluation. The interviews in this evaluation were biased and the events were untrue. Essentially, the family members lied or received their erroneous information from the mother. So it was just propaganda spread by the mother to the family members. The fact is the family members had not witnessed the events they had described to the psychologist, yet the psychologist chose to believe them, and this caused my client to receive an unfavorable evaluation. This was a case where the psychologist ignored issues favorable to my client and emphasized issues favorable to the mother.

Unfortunately, this is not uncommon in custody disputes. Either the psychologist is biased or they didn't go the extra mile to secure the facts. Collateral information in this case was proving the family members really had no knowledge of the alleged events. We needed to secure the true story from other witnesses the psychologist didn't interview. When this happens, it can be embarrassing to the psychologist. We simply had no choice but to interview as many unbiased witnesses as possible to secure the truth. Furthermore, we needed to prove that the mother defied the psychologist's advice regarding a new relationship. This was easy because the mother had the boyfriend over every night when her child was present. We simply photographed the boyfriend's car at the mother's home and kept a record of the activity at the home.

Proving a psychologist is biased or incompetent is like walking on egg shells. Some attorneys will not attack the integrity of the psychologist, but sometimes this is necessary. The psychologist in this case had a way to save face because the mother defied the advice regarding a new relationship. However, to make the psychologist aware of the erroneous information, it would be necessary to get the psychologist to change the recommendation. In this case, we chose to depose the psychologist and asked questions regarding our new evidence.

The father wanted 50 percent of the time with his child. Because the child was not yet in school, we believed this was a realistic request. Not only that, but we interviewed and obtained signed affidavits from unbiased witnesses regarding visitational interference and other discrepancies the psychologist chose to ignore.

In this case, we also used the other option of hiring another psychologist to critique the evaluation. The evaluation included psychological testing—the MMPI-2. Ironically, the psychologist failed to disclose the test results in the report filed to the court. We believed the psychologist purposely left this information out of the report because it didn't help the mother.

The mother was definitely difficult and seemed, in our opinion, to have personality disorders. The psychologist was a woman in this case and was obviously an advocate of mothers, which hurt my client in the evaluation. The psychologist was selective in what was revealed in the report to benefit the mother. There were police reports that proved visitational interference by the mother, but the psychologist ignored them.

She interviewed a few of our witnesses and actually admitted to them that the mother was difficult and even raged at her employees at her office. The psychologist even told the witnesses she was going to give my client 50 percent with his child. Once I learned this, I obtained sworn statements from the witnesses stating what the psychologists told them. This could have put the psychologist in even deeper water in court because if we went to court, we could embarrass the psychologist and destroy her credibility. The psychologist would be put in the compromising situation of having to say our witnesses were liars. That posed even another problem for the psychologist because these witnesses were not family members and they would have credibility with the court.

So the psychologist was in jeopardy of losing her grand reputation with the judges. Because the psychologist failed to include the results of the MMPI-2, we subpoenaed her file. This would include her notes, interviews, and test results. Ironically, the notes contradicted her report. The psychologist took meticulous notes that described a borderline personality disorder of the mother. Either the psychologist mixed up her report or she was dishonest. Either way, our new psychologist could look through her notes, reports, and test results to contradict her evaluation.

Without hiring a new psychologist to critique the evaluation, we would be in danger of losing, because the courts rely on these so-called experts. Many professionals are so arrogant they won't back off even when they are wrong. But by having another expert, the psychologist was in danger of humiliation. Or she just simply needed to revisit her evaluation and use the mother's boyfriend as a way to save face and change the evaluation to benefit my client.

This psychologist really had an ego problem, as we discovered when we read her notes. The psychologist actually wrote "Ph.D." at the end of every one of her notes. We were dealing with a serious ego and our chance of having her change her evaluation was probably a long shot. The attorney and I discussed a strategy and we decided to take the mother's deposition. We knew we would be able to get the mother to say some outrageous things that would benefit our client. The mother's attorney had already sent letters telling us the mother didn't believe the father should have overnight visitation. This is really unheard of in custody cases unless the father has a serious drug, alcohol, or psychological problem. In this case, the father was quite normal. We also believed we could contradict the psychologist's report by going over every line in the report that was untrue.

Of course, there is always the problem of people lying in depositions—and we fully believed the mother would lie. However, we did our homework and took sworn statements that contradicted the report as well as what the mother had said about the father. We could submit the affidavits or sworn statements as exhibits. The mother would be put in the position of having to call our witnesses liars, which in this case were her own neighbors. She would also have to call the police officers who reported the visitational interference liars as well.

Our last weapon was the boyfriend. She would have to lie about him, too. If she lied about the boyfriend, we would simply show the photographs of him at the house. Because I had run a motor vehicle check on the vehicle, we knew his name. All of this information would be on the record. After we embarrassed the mother for all her problems and lies, we could then send a copy of the deposition to the court-appointed psychologist in an attempt to persuade her to change her evaluation in this case.

The psychologist already knew we had another expert critiquing her work. Next, we could depose the psychologist and embarrass her if she didn't change her mind. In this case the psychologist did back off and changed her evaluation. The boyfriend issue really hit home. When the psychologist changed her evaluation, she gave my client about 40 percent with his child instead of the 50 percent we wanted.

This was a case where the mother wanted it all. She wanted sole custody, the house, the equity in the house, and all of the furniture. Because we live in a community property state, she was only entitled to 50 percent of the assets. What the psychologist failed to understand was that the mother was willing to go to trial no matter what the custody evaluation was because she wanted sole custody.

My client told me he took notes of the conversations he had with the psychologist, which was very beneficial. The psychologist told my client that because of the mother's irrational behavior, she was in danger of losing custody if she went to trial. Even though the psychologist was willing to admit to my client that the mother was irrational, she gave her 75 percent of the time with the child.

Essentially, the psychologist was playing God. She was trying to save the mother by giving a favorable arrangement in an attempt to thwart the trial. The psychologist was giving the mother custody to prevent her from losing custody in court. This is a disgrace. This psychologist deserved to have a complaint filed against her with the psychology board for her bias.

But the psychologist underestimated the mother. Because the mother's father was paying the tab, it was all or nothing in this case. So the case was going to trial. The mother's stubbornness to go to trial was really a tactical mistake made by her attorney.

If the judge felt the mother was too hysterical or too controlling, she was in danger of losing altogether. In other words, the judge might see the pattern of her behavior. The judge might see she was not willing to share the child with the father. In fact, the judge might decide joint custody was not an option because of her need to control and have it all. In cases where parents cannot get along, joint custody is not a good option because the parents continue to fight over the children even after the divorce or custody settlement.

Unfortunately, the courts are not tough enough in this regard. Psychologists and judges take the position of not allowing either parent to have too much power over the children by rendering a joint custody arrangement. But in this case we could show a pattern of the mother denying visitation as well as wanting all the community assets.

The mother was uncompromising, which in court doesn't go over well. The courts are set up for compromise. Parenting is compromising and sharing the children. This mother didn't want to compromise at all. That's why this case was headed to trial.

Can behavior of the parents arguing over assets affect the custody arrangement? Yes! If the psychologist chooses to consider behavior. In this case, the psychologist was choosing to ignore the mother's irrational behavior regarding nearly every angle of the divorce. The father was willing to compromise and raise the child 40 percent of the time. He had always maintained his position to share the child. But his attorney could always switch gears in court and ask the judge for sole custody because of the mother's behavior. Not all cases get turned around like this one. Often the attorney will not challenge the psychological evaluation. Our attorney did because we had the facts on our side. It was just a matter of pointing them out in a logical and thorough manner. My client did go to trial and he was awarded 50-percent custody as well as 50 percent of the financial assets.

Here are some Do's and Don'ts regarding your psychological evaluation.

Do:

1. Read the questions carefully and answer them truthfully.

2. Listen to the psychologist's questions carefully and answer them truthfully.

3. Prepare a diary regarding your life with your spouse and the problems you are having.

4. Have your attorney supply as much evidence as possible that proves your case to the psychologist.

5. Maintain a professional appearance and demeanor with the psychologist at all times.

6. Refer to your child as "our" child rather than "my" child.

7. Show your concern for your child's best interest to the psychologist.

Don't:

1. Tell the psychologist how to do their job.

2. Use psychology labels or descriptions.

3. Buddy up to the psychologist in an attempt to persuade them that you are the best parent.

4. Ever call your spouse names.

When taking psychological tests, you need to read the statements carefully. Pay close attention to words such as sometimes, always, never, often, frequently, nearly, almost, and usually. These words may have an impact on your answers. So read carefully before answering.

When talking to the psychologist, you want to be as positive as possible even though you are in a highly emotional state. You want to be a problem solver or a willing participant to help solve your differences with your spouse.

Listen to the psychologist, because they will often want to push your buttons. So think before you answer.

The Case of the Pool Shark

This is one of those cases that happens to me every once in a while when I learn about another culture. In this case, it was pool. Bonnie[1], a woman I knew from politics, called me and said she needed to hire me. At first I thought it was for political purposes. But when I met with her she explained her situation. She told me she was getting married and moving to Texas.

I said, "Best wishes. When are you going?"

She replied, "When the court allows me to leave." She told me her daughter's father did not know about the move. This was smart on her part because she had not lost the element of surprise. She said she

---

1. Name has been changed to protect privacy

needed the court's permission to move according to her custody agreement.

Bonnie was a polite, sophisticated woman no older than 30. I had no idea she had ever been married, but I did know she had a five-year-old daughter, Megan[2]. She told me her ex-husband, Jack[3], had served time in jail for driving under the influence of alcohol. She believed he still drank, even in front of his daughter during his visitation.

So the objective was to prove two things:

1. We needed to catch Jack drinking and driving, therefore violating his probation.

2. We needed to prove he was driving and drinking with Megan present.

Jack had visitation one night a week and every other weekend overnight. I had to ask Bonnie the obvious question: "Does he drive to pick up your daughter?"

She said yes. Boy! This was easy already. Although Jack told her he had a driver's license, I was skeptical. I knew that most people who serve time for DUI have felony convictions, which means a long waiting period to apply for a driver's license. They essentially have two hurdles: the first is to meet the terms of their probation, whatever they may be. I have seen DUI felons go three years or longer to apply for a driver's license.

The second hurdle is to convince the state licensing board that you deserve a license. In other words just because you have served your time and met the terms of your probation is not enough to get a new license. The courts convict you but the licensing boards regulate. I knew there was no guarantee Jack could have convinced a licensing board he was off alcohol and was clean and sober to drive.

---

2. Name has been changed to protect privacy
3. Name has been changed to protect privacy

I told Bonnie the first thing I wanted to do was videotape her ex-husband picking up Megan. I told her I wanted to preserve that as evidence ASAP because if he had bugged her phone or got wind somehow she was going to hire me, we might miss our chance. He could suddenly turn over a new can—I mean *leaf*—and stop driving. Again the element of surprise is critical in this kind of situation.

Because of my time constraint and my concern of preserving the evidence, I performed an activity check on Jack. Normally I like to collect intelligence on a subject prior to surveillance or interviewing witnesses. This way I am armed with some background information. When I sort through lawsuits, divorce records, driving records, or other sources, it usually gives a clearer picture of both sides of the situation. This protects my clients and me, and improves my ability to achieve results.

Frankly, I don't care about protecting myself legally (unlike attorneys who basically represent themselves first, while their clients are somewhere down the totem pole). I have been in litigation before and I will be again. It's a fact of life and part of business. In my business every time I get results for my client somebody else is on the other end of my performance.

Gathering information is so important in these cases and so important in our lives. Let me give you a couple of examples. What is the most important commodity in your life? Money? Wrong! Time is most important because you only have so much time to live—period. So if you are going to date somebody, you are going to spend and share the most important commodity in your life—time. When was the last time you saw somebody who just started dating a new fling and they knew nothing about this person? The next thing you know they are living together or maybe they get married and have a baby or two. Then a few years later they get a nasty divorce. Basically they discover they never knew each other or that their values were different—if they even had values to begin with. Bottom line: It gives me a job. America is reactive. Now if a person investigated their potential boyfriend or girlfriend, they might run for the hills from that person after they discover the truth.

I have talked with women about this before and many of them say the same thing. They simply believe this kind of research and attitude isn't romantic and destroys the process of intimacy—that is, for the men reading this book, getting to know each other without an agenda or ulterior motive. Of course I couldn't disagree more. These same women who didn't believe in researching a possible mate or date are the same people who call a hundred different stores to compare prices on clothes. Or they are the same people who price numerous designers to decorate their homes. You see, when money is involved it's different. Of course really it isn't different because in every relationship there is time, materials, and money. And there are no exceptions. Somebody's got to pay for entertainment. For some men out there it is actually less expensive to pay child support than date on a monthly basis, meaning if a man dated a woman and she tried to trap him by getting pregnant, then paying child support is obviously less expensive than getting married. If it gets to this point, the relationship has probably been destroyed. So in some minds it is a less expensive alternative to pay child support.

When I sort through these files, it gives me an opportunity to piece the case together, to see weaknesses and strengths. Not all investigators have the analytical skills I possess in custody. Nevertheless all intelligence relies on analysis and data collection. Analysis is imperative to converting raw data into information. The raw data is collected in the field in numerous ways. The best way is HUMINT, an intelligence term meaning the physical surveillance of having operatives get the data first hand. There's not enough of it. Lawyers rely on subpoenas for information and the government relies on satellites.

Anyway, back to the case: I had to preserve the evidence ASAP because Jack was getting visitation for the weekend. Bonnie called me on a Thursday so I quickly set up surveillance on his visitation for the next day. Without knowing his legal situation, I videotaped Jack as he picked up his daughter. I figured if he doesn't have a license and he is driving, we at least have him on that and we can preserve the evidence.

But it got better—a lot better. I followed him directly to a pool hall about five miles from his ex-wife's house.

Unfortunately, I wasn't dressed for the occasion. Pool halls are cliquish. Customers know as soon as you walk in if you're a regular, a cop, or a sucker waiting to be hustled. Because I don't play pool and in this hall it was only for money, I ordered a beer. I was dressed in jeans but I looked too nice for this dump. I sat at the bar and scanned the wall of this pool hall. This place had serious players. There were trophies surrounding the bar area and across the room there were shelves stacked with trophies.

I made no eye contact with the subject. He was playing pool and drinking a beer, Megan was sitting near the pool table eating popcorn. It was Friday night—I guessed that was her dinner. I sat with the drunks at the bar and listened to their hard luck stories. They were rugged men who worked construction labor in Arizona. The heat is so intense in the summer that laborers are up by 3 a.m. and finished by 2 p.m. I know. I did it the summer I graduated from high school. I swung a pick for a summer. What an experience. I worked with mostly ex-cons. They took me to bars after work and we would drink beer for a couple hours, eat, and crash. The next day was the same drill.

It was fall and the weather was cool. I could have easily concealed a weapon under my jacket if necessary. I was the only man at the bar without tattoos or a criminal record. In fact I'm sure I was the only man in the bar with a security clearance from serving in the United States Army. I counted beers because I wanted to see how many he would suck down before they drove home. I counted seven and by 10:30, then he took Megan to his house. I grabbed a gut bomb from a fast-food place and called it a night. I knew the next time I went to the pool hall I would have to dress down. That meant beat-up clothes, caps, and no shaving. My next order of business would be data collection of the subject's driving records.

After going through his criminal records, I realized it was even better for us than I anticipated. Over the past 10 years, this guy had been charged and convicted of four DUIs. He spent more than 400 days incarcerated in the past six years. Part of his probation was no driving or alcohol for three years. A year had past so he had two years left to abstain. This was sad because after reading through court documents, I got the impression he was a nice guy. There were numerous letters from people to the judge as character references. This is standard, but these letters had some content. At 43, Jack was quite a bit older than his ex, who was 30. According to the court record, he was a blue-collar worker his whole life with no living relatives. While Bonnie wore a suit to work, this guy got his hands dirty. It wasn't difficult to see why they were no longer married. But what I couldn't figure out was how they got together in the first place. That's probably another book.

Jack was really in deep doo-doo. Not only had he violated his probation of driving and drinking, but also he was drinking and driving with his daughter. But as I told my client, we still needed to show a pattern of behavior. Essentially according to Arizona law to establish a lifestyle of behavior you must show a pattern, a repetition. So we needed not only to make certified copies of his criminal record to show the judge, but I needed to observe him drinking and driving several more times.

I decided to follow Jack after work on Mondays, Wednesdays, and Fridays. The following week I would follow him on Tuesdays and Thursdays. That way I covered the whole work week. He worked for a tire company and went to the pool hall every day after work. In fact, instead of following him from work to the pool hall, I decided to limit my chances of getting caught. So I just met him there every day. Actually I would beat him there and remove his notion of being followed (I cover this under "Techniques of Surveillance").

Because I spent so much time in the pool hall, I needed a character. So I used the name Lyle, which was my uncle's name. My story was simple. I had just separated from the Army and I needed a job. Which wasn't far from the truth anyway. I had a short haircut, almost shaved head (high and tight). I let my beard grow a little and wore hole-y jeans, a jean jacket, a cap, and my field boots from the Army. I got these in boot camp and they were broken in and soft as glove leather.

The bartender was an attractive brunette with large breasts and a small waist, the type of woman who poses on tool part calendars. She was trashy but sexy. She and I talked a lot. I knew her life story. And she knew everyone's story but mine. I think she liked me because I didn't talk like the others. I had a college education, spoke the Queen's English, and didn't swear in her presence. In fact as time progressed she told me she wanted to have an affair with me. I played along just long enough to get her license plate, her full name, and address. I figured she served my subject's beers nightly and she might have to testify. Later she found out my real name and she called me. She wasn't mad because I had lied to her. Instead she seemed even more interested.

When I went to court, I testified that I watched Jack violate his probation over the course of approximately six weeks. I testified he drank a minimum of five to eleven beers every time I observed him, drank and drove with his daughter, and had a revoked driver's license.

Bonnie's attorney supplied the judge with a certified copy of Jack's dismal driving record. I also told the judge Jack drove a company truck while engaging in this activity. The attorney, on my advice, pointed out Jack put his daughter at risk by driving because if there were any injuries, the insurance on the company vehicle would probably deny coverage because he was not a licensed driver.

I actually had another option on this case. I could have contacted Jack's probation officer and had him back in the slammer. Some probation officers are useless and some are good. But with a five-year old involved, I believe the probation officer would have helped us. But Bonnie chose not to handle the case this way. Jack had a reasonably good relationship with his daughter but he had a serious alcohol problem. I hope he gets help and doesn't kill somebody. On a better note, the judge granted my client and her daughter safe passage to Texas. I still get thank you cards and pictures on Christmas from them.

Neglect

When I set out to prove neglect, I begin by examining the day in the life of the parent. For example, most parents work approximately eight hours a day. And most parents sleep approximately eight hours a day. That leaves eight hours a day to spend with their children, right? Well, you know as well as I do children go to school and go to bed early in a good home. So sometimes I don't even need to examine a parent's time with their children during the week because they spend very little time with them. However, on the weekend when parents have the time to spend with the children and choose not to—that's neglect. And this can occur at any time that they have the option of seeing them.

I worked a case where a woman was a haircutter and she had flexible hours. She basically worked Tuesday through Friday and Saturday mornings. But she partied Thursday through Monday. Thursdays and Fridays she would go out to a happy hour and get drunk. Saturday was a date or drinks with a group of people. This woman was a groupie for a local band so tracking her was easy. I would simply show up wherever the band was playing, count her drinks, and document the time she spent away from her children. On one occasion, I sat with her and bought a round of drinks for everyone at the table.

On Sundays she played golf and drank beer. She was having affairs with numerous men—one of them a golf pro. So she would play golf on Sundays and Mondays. During football season, she would drink at a sports bar while watching Monday Night Football. When you compute how much time she spent with her children, it was almost zero.

Records showed she would take her children to childcare on Mondays, even when she didn't work. On Thursday through Saturday she employed babysitters so she could go out. Of course, it's no surprise she failed to get one child to school on time. Why? Because one child would go to childcare and the other child would go to elementary school and this was complicated by the fact she slept in hung over.

This is the kind of case I like to work because I use interviews as my weapon of choice and it saves my client money. By getting the license plates of the vehicles at her home, I was able to document who she slept with and who the babysitters were. It took surveillance, which can be expensive, but sometimes neighbors are helpful or you can spot check the vehicles. This means I drive by and write down the license plate numbers. I then can interview the people later to create a picture of what the parent's lifestyle is all about. When I finally put together the neglect of this case, it was depressing like many of my cases.

Sometimes when you set out to prove neglect, it becomes abuse. Or the fact there is abuse or neglect often shows a cause-effect relationship with alcohol or drug abuse, or in some cases even sex addiction. But all in all when you plug in the times of the day and evenings the parent could be with their children but choose not to be—this builds a case for neglect. This is what a court-appointed psychologist should examine.

Why have custody of children if you're not going to spend time with them? On the other hand, the physical neglect becomes mental neglect. If the parent is spending no time with their child, ultimately this may become mental abuse. Children need attention, discipline, and positive reinforcement.

Personality Disorders

Personality is basically the pattern or traits and behaviors that charac-
terize an individual. A healthy adult personality simply complies with
society's expectations. A healthy adult is able to adjust to the changes of
their life cycle. As they get older, there are some things they cannot do.
For example, as they get older their athletic abilities decrease. However,
healthy adults adapt to the changing demands or limitations associated
with life stages. To the contrary, some adults establish patterns of
behavior that are ill equipped to become productive in society. Some
adults become warped over time and are unable to perform in society or
as parents. These parents might be diagnosed as having a **personality
disorder**. For our purposes, personality disorders are immature or distorted personality patterns. These parents persistently perceive the
world in a distorted way. This certainly doesn't mean they are not intelligent, but they are usually unable to perform optimally in society.
Their character traits often overshadow their talents.

Personality disorder is a broad science, and I'm certainly no psycho-
therapist. But I have enough experience to know that some people have
personality disorders that may affect their ability to be good parents.
There are several types of personality disorders with distinct characteristics that may overlap by definition. Some parents have a combination
of personality traits that may fit more than one personality disorder.
For example, a parent may be narcissistic and a sociopath. For the purposes of acquiring custody, the court-appointed psychologist will
attempt to discover any personality disorder a parent may have.

Psychologists believe that by determining the personality and character traits of a parent, they can better determine who would be best as the custodial parent. The psychologist attempts to discover this by administering the MMPI-2 to the parent.

I have consulted on hundreds of custody cases and I can tell you the MMPI-2 is not foolproof. Psychologists make mistakes evaluating parents every day, though they'll tell you the MMPI-2 is a very reliable test. I will tell you that on many occasions, it isn't. I certainly would not want to stake my life or my children's lives on this test. Yes, it is true psychologists use other types of testing to determine custody. But the fact is they rely on this test more than any other and parents fool psychologists often. Unfortunately, our children pay for their inability to determine the truth.

This is why I have all my clients do their own diary and independent investigation to paint a picture of the other parent's personality. The evaluation performed by the overwhelming majority of court-appointed psychologists is just not thorough enough. The MMPI-2 and a few interviews (even some psychologists admit their evaluation isn't enough analysis to be thorough) just isn't enough. Yet this is the way parents are evaluated to determine custody. Ironically, my clients have difficulty determining if their spouses have a personality disorder because they live with them or have lived with them. When you are living in the situation, your objectivity is sometimes non-existent. You may think your spouse's behavior is actually normal because you probably have nothing to compare it to, until you are not living with them.

If somebody has a personality disorder or character traits that make life difficult for them and everyone around them, you may say, "So what?" Because psychologists recommend custody based on personality, it becomes very important.

We all have some traits that are not perfect, but the psychologist is looking for traits that are extreme enough to affect good parenting. Sometimes these extreme traits don't even surface until a custody battle escalates, because many parents consider their children a possession. This is when you see parents at their worst. One parent believes they are the only parent for the child. They refuse to accept that the other parent has any rights. This attitude or perception is more common with mothers. Many mothers don't think men have instincts to be a large part of a child's life; or that they are incapable of raising a child.

The personality disorder is not always going to win or lose your case, but it is certainly a big part of it. If you look at the whole picture, you may discover a lot about your spouse or opponent. When you look at all of the problems in your relationship, you might see that many of the problems were because of personality. You may see extreme vanity or a personality that feels the world only revolves around them. You may see a person who has to control everyone and everything around them, or a person who never compromises. You may see a person who constantly lies, or a person with an alcohol or drug problem. This is significant because people with alcohol or drug problems almost always have a personality disorder. They are turning to alcohol or drugs to escape.

Psychologists know alcohol and drug abuse is an escape from other problems, but not all psychologists know how to look for substance abuse. However, I will attest that most court-appointed psychologists know how to find personality disorders. The only problem is that often they don't find one when there is one. Some personality types are so subtle from a testing point of view they go undetected. Yet the personality disorder could still be extreme. This is another reason why a diary is so important. It helps the psychologist focus on the personality type of the other spouse.

Now that you know that a personality type or disorder is critical to child custody, let's examine some of the basic character traits of personality disorders common in custody cases.

Borderline Personality Disorder

Impulsiveness, inappropriate and uncontrollable anger, drastic mood shifts, chronic feelings of boredom or suicide, unstable interpersonal relationships.

Borderline Personality Disorder is difficult to detect by a court-appointed psychologist. The reason is that the symptoms of this disorder are subtle. In a case I worked, the psychologist didn't deny custody to the parent who had a borderline personality disorder. Sometimes the borderline personality disorder isn't extreme enough to deny custody. Nevertheless, in my experience I have found people with borderline personality disorder just as difficult to deal with as any other disorder.

I can't think of a better reason to deny custody to someone than suicide. If a person is borderline, they may be suicidal. Or they may have the potential to murder their own children. Obviously, a person like this is a threat to their children. I have also seen parents with borderline personality disorder yell at their children for no reason and with no warning. From a parenting point of view, this confuses children. From a custody point of view, this parent may not be the best alternative for custody of the children. Naturally, proof is essential to winning your case. If you can prove through witnesses that the parent is borderline, your case will be helped. Interviewing witnesses who have witnessed these violent outbursts is essential. They may be neighbors, babysitters, childcare workers, or teachers.

Anti-Social Personality Disorder or Sociopath

Lacks morals or ethics, shameless, manipulative, conduct problems as a child, no guilt, deceitful, theft.

Sociopaths can be difficult to identify from interviews because this type of person will be anyone you want them to be. They will assume an identity to gain control or get the upper hand. As a criminal investigator, I have encountered my share of sociopaths. They can be very intelligent and manipulative people. You can never underestimate a sociopath because they have little or no guilt. They are potentially deadly individuals. I'm not saying all sociopaths are capable of murder, but some are. In custody cases, a parent who is a sociopath is dangerous because some of them will teach their children to lie, cheat, and steal.

In custody cases, the sociopath will attempt to win at all costs. They will scheme, lie, and manipulate everyone around them. In one case I worked, the court-appointed psychologist was able to determine clinically that a mother was in fact a sociopath. Unfortunately, this was only after the mother had filed three false police reports against the father. In one instance, a police detective called my client and wanted to interview him. The police detective wanted to actually interview him at his home rather than the police station or at his office. I believe the police really wanted to arrest my client. The mother was a sociopath and she was attractive and convincing. Even the detective had no real evidence, but it appeared he was still willing to arrest my client. I told my client to tell the detective he could interview him at his attorney's office.

Ironically, the police detective testified at our trial for us because the police report was false, though they didn't charge the woman for filing a false police report. Because legitimately there is a lot of domestic violence, the police tend to be biased towards women. Most likely a man who files a false police report would be charged.

Narcissistic Personality Disorder

Self love, exaggerated concern with self, oriented toward superficial interests, unable to remain in love, unable to take the perspective of others, self-promoting, lack of empathy.

Narcissism works hand in hand with sociopathic behavior. Both disorders are promiscuous and lack empathy. Simply put, they both only see things through their own eyes. The world revolves around them. Narcissistic people are vain to a fault.

Again, someone with this disorder cannot be underestimated because they look out for Number One at almost all costs. Based on my experience, the only thing you can do with sociopaths or narcissists is contain them. You can never rest around these people; they need to fear consequences for their actions. If they lie, cheat, steal, or manipulate, they must be punished. Punishment could include reduced visitation, attorney's fees, etc. You must have a plan to punish the parent with the personality disorder.

Dependent Personality Disorder

Difficulty in separating in a relationship, discomfort at being alone, subordinates needs in order to keep others involved in relationships, indecisiveness, panic of being alone, builds life around other people, lacks self-confidence.

This disorder is really easy to identify. For example, you might have a friend who never calls unless they are between relationships. As long as they are in a relationship, they are all right. But as soon as they break up they are on your doorstep to avoid being alone. They are usually dominated by their relationship. Their spouse or partner makes all the decisions for them. In custody cases, this can be detrimental to the children because the parent lets their relationship dominate their priorities. The children are not first in line for attention. These people in my opinion make bad leaders. Consequently, the children receive no order or stability to their lives. Often their relationships fail, leaving the children with unstable parents. The parent with dependency personality disorder often replaces their spouse, which confuses the children. In custody battles, interviewing neighbors and former partners to show instability can prove this. The parent with dependency personality disorder may marry often. Researching the marriage license and divorce records will reveal their instability and panic of being alone.

Obsessive-Compulsive Disorder

Excessive concern with order, rules, and trivial details, perfectionist, lack of expressiveness and warmth, difficulty in relaxing and having fun.

In custody, a parent with obsessive-compulsive personality disorder may be too hard on their children. They may put too many demands on their children and put too much stress on them to perform.

This disorder may not be a reason to deny custody unless the parent is so extreme it damages the child. Unfortunately, many parents put no demands on their children, so in some cases, the parent with obsessive-compulsive personality disorder may actually add balance to the parenting. However, just because you discipline or maintain order with your children doesn't mean you have obsessive-compulsive disorder. In many cases I have worked, one parent may demand discipline and order from their children while the other parent lets the children manipulate and rule the house. So the child has difficulty adjusting from one home to the next. In a better scenario, the divorced parents agree on how to parent so the transition from one parent to the other is smoother.

Manic-Depressive Psychosis or Bipolar Personality Disorder

Mood swings, hyper excitability, extreme elation, flight of ideas, depression, suicidal impulses, sadness, unresponsiveness.

I have seen this disorder hidden from people in relationships for months at a time. So naturally, if a person with bipolar disorder can hide it from a girlfriend or boyfriend, they can certainly hide it from a psychologist. Unlike some disorders, this is treatable with mood altering drugs. That is, if you can get the person to take medication on a regular basis. Some people with bipolar disorder are in denial that they have it, making it difficult to treat them.

People with bipolar disorder may be able to fool people for a while, but they really have to compensate to go undetected. However, ultimately they will break down and the disorder will appear. From a custody point of view, people with bipolar disorder will confuse their children because of the mood swings. Again, like borderline personality disorder, bipolar disorder has suicidal impulses. This obviously puts the children at risk. However, interviewing people in their past relationships will shed light on their disorder.

Alcoholism and Drug Abuse

Alcoholism has been researched and studied for many years. This subject is best identified and explained by professionals. However, in many instances parents and grandparents are far removed from alcoholism. And they simply don't know what to look for to even know if a person has an alcohol problem. I have found through my investigations in custody disputes that alcoholics and people with alcohol problems are different in methods of abuse. Some people with alcohol problems like to get drunk and party with their friends. And they don't do much to hide it. This is their chosen lifestyle and it can be very relevant in custody cases. Yet people often will hide from their problems through alcohol or drugs. Some people choose not to drink at home, so identifying their problem can sometimes be difficult. Instead they use events, concerts, parties, and holidays to get drunk. So the places they consume alcohol can vary. Proving their abuse may require surveillance or witnesses to establish their abuse.

Some people drink at bars on the way home from work, and use business as an excuse to indulge. Obviously this can destroy a person's physical and mental health over time. If I am working a custody case and I want to prove an alcohol problem, I like to catch the parent drinking and driving in the car with children. The reason people drink to excess is a question experts have pondered for some time now. Some say people are predisposed to drinking genetically. But most psychotherapists agree alcohol and drug abuse is a symptom of another problem. It may be insecurity or low self-esteem. Whatever the reason, it takes its toll on a family.

I classify alcoholics in a different category for investigation because alcoholics will hide their drinking problems. They will hide the alcohol in their house or car to avoid detection. I have worked cases where I've followed the parent to lunch while they were working to prove they drink every day at lunch. On occasion I have found that a parent will go to lunch alone so their co-workers will not detect their problem. I have investigated auto accidents and found airplane bottles of liquor in their glove compartments. And of course many times I have searched the trash of parents' homes to prove alcoholism. These are things you need to look for in alcoholics. I have also sized up the parent by physical size to determine if alcohol is their problem. Some people have red faces or they are many pounds overweight. Alcohol for many people increases their weight.

Like alcohol, drug abuse has different signs. Today the drug of choice is methamphetamine. This drug is made in homes. It is not grown like marijuana or cocaine. Methamphetamine is often referred to as crystal. This drug is popular because it is relatively easy to make and easy to buy. Some would agree it is similar to cocaine, but it is much cheaper. So this drug crosses all socio-economic classes. I have found that people who indulge in this highly addictive drug tend to be very thin. I have also seen a sickly yellowing of the skin on crystal addicts.

To prove drug abuse, you have options other than surveillance or a trash search. You can drug test parents for drug abuse if a judge will order a test.

The Truth about Drug Testing

Again, this is a subject best explained by professionals. But you need to know your options to prove chronic drug abuse. The courts in this country have been using urine analysis for many years. But unfortunately, drugs in the body can be a short-lived event. In many cases, urine analysis can only detect the use of drugs three to five days from the time it was used. So if a parent used cocaine or crystal on Friday evening and the test is given the following Wednesday the test might prove negative.

However, if a parent is a chronic marijuana user, the test may detect as far back as 30 days. But I wouldn't bet on it. Unbelievably, people advertise in newspapers selling their clean urine to parents who might take this test. There are also vitamins on the market today that people have claimed can clean the urine to avoid detection.

This is why I believe the best test is a hair test. There are some labs in the country that test hair for chronic drug use. A notable case is Washington D.C. Mayor Marion Barry. The FBI performed a hair test to detect cocaine use during their investigation of the Mayor. You would have to contact a competent lab to learn more about hair testing, but in some cases hair tests can detect chronic use of drugs for several months.

The Case of the Doctor's House Call

This is a twisted story about two people with complicated needs. It's amazing this story ended the way it did. An attorney referred me to this case. My client was a doctor. He said his wife was 36, overweight, and wetted the bed. He told me she was an alcoholic. From his emotional state she had put this guy through hell. He was so bitter about the breakup. I think he was more upset at himself than he was at her. This guy told me some sick things about his wife that I'd rather not talk about.

Bob[1] moved out of a nice home. He said he slept in his office for two months before he could muster the money to rent himself a home. Of course his wife stayed in the home and the children remained with her. She had a job and they had a nanny. The nanny was there about two months before the doctor moved out. When I interviewed Bob, I met

---

1. Name has been changed to protect privacy

another doctor at his office who worked for him. I didn't pay much attention to this guy at first, but later it would prove to be important.

In this case, Bob and his wife, Doris[2], had a court appointed psychologist, who I knew personally from other cases. He had a good reputation for recommending sole custody to one of the parents, particularly in cases where the parents couldn't agree on anything.

My mission in this case was pretty clear: I needed to prove Doris was a lush. To accomplish this task, I told Bob I would need to catch her drinking and driving and possibly driving with the kids in the car. I also told him I would need to go through her trash at his former home to see if she throws away her alcohol of choice. In this case, it was white wine in a big way.

Unbeknownst to me, Bob's associate was listening through the door during our consultation. Well that scum was having an affair with Doris. Naturally he called Doris and told her "Guy the P.I. Legend" was on the case. What the scum didn't know was that I wasn't going to begin the case for two weeks. First of all I wanted to check the story out by reviewing the court records in the divorce. And I wanted to audit the home or, as a burglar would say, case the place.

Now I know what you're thinking: She knows an investigator is on the case so she's going to change her behavior, and we aren't going to find anything on this woman. As I always say, she'll be going to church, wearing long skirts, firing the babysitter, and staying home at night. Well that does happen often. But take note of this story because this is an example of a person who is chemically dependent with a serious drinking problem. She knew I was going after her trash—but she drank so much wine when she came home from work that the bottles stacked up. For a while, according to the nanny I interviewed, Doris was putting her trash in her car and dumping it somewhere else. Except after two weeks she got tired of doing that.

Doris was already worn out. She thought I was following her to work, to lunch, and home again. Doris was taking evasive measures to

---

2.   Name has been changed to protect privacy

avoid me for two weeks. Well by the time I began actively working the case, she had dropped her guard. And now it was time for me to punch. In the next two weeks, I found 29 empty bottles of wine in her trash. Some of the bottles were liter size. I found TV dinners and Bob's clothes thrown in the trash.

Next I followed Doris to lunch. This was so easy it made my teeth hurt. People are creatures of habit. And Doris ate lunch every day at one of three restaurants located in a shopping mall less than a mile from her office.

Doris suspected she was being followed to lunch, but I wasn't caught. I would sit at lunch and watch her chug a glass of wine, and then she would order lunch and three more glasses of wine. Then Doris would hit a happy hour after work at a place near her home and drink three or four more glasses of wine. Doris was always alone. She didn't want her co-workers to go to lunch with her because they would see she was an alcoholic. Doris had no friends except for the bartenders at the places she would frequent.

After Doris pounded her wine, she would then go and pick up her children from childcare. I went to lunch with Doris about ten times, randomly following her on various weekdays. The pattern for her was drinking every day at lunch. Ironically I followed her one day and Bob's associate, Dr. Score[3], picked her up at work to go to lunch. He drove around in circles to lose me. I just hung back and met them at one of the three restaurants I knew they would go. I walked in and looked for Doris drinking so I could document this and I left without being seen. Dr. Score was married and fornicating with Doris a couple of times a month.

I only followed Doris to happy hours a few times. Between her lunch drinking, a few happy hours, and picking up the kids under the influence, plus 29 bottles of wine out of her trash bagged and tagged—the party was over! The drinking problem had been established.

---

3. Name has been changed to protect privacy

My second order of business was to interview a former nanny and record her on video or audio. She avoided me when I went to her apartment, but I finally got her on the phone and taped an hour-long interview, replete with the kind of goods people in my business relish. This interview buried Doris. The nanny was only 19, but she had better parenting skills than Doris would ever have. You see, Doris is sick, and sick people do stupid things to their children. Although it may not be intentional, the damage is done.

The nanny told me the house was filthy and Doris let the kids eat off the floor. She said Doris had no groceries in the home except for white wine. She often fed the children peanut butter and jelly or had pizza delivered. The nanny said Doris would leave the nine-month-old baby in the bathtub alone while she would curl her hair in the other room. She also knew about Dr. Score and the affair. The nanny also told me the vindictive things she did to Bob, like disconnecting his utilities at his office and sabotaging his car. There are a lot of evil people out there and Doris was one of them.

Ironically, Doris did well in her interview with the court appointed psychologist. She convinced the psychologist she was not a drinker and was an attentive parent. I think one of the reasons for this was my client was bitter and obnoxious, plus his ego clashed with the psychologist's. But the day my report was turned over to Doris' attorney and the psychologist, Doris checked into alcohol rehabilitation. What a coincidence! I guess her attorney thought this was good advice.

Actually it was an act of desperation. She thought she would just go to rehabilitation for 30 days, be cured, and instantly be a good mother. That wasn't the case. Not only that, but she lost instant credibility with the psychologist. One thing psychologists don't like is lying, and of course they don't like to be wrong either. When Doris checked into rehabilitation, she blamed her husband for everything, naturally. But she did admit she drank two gallons of wine per day.

We subpoenaed her records at the drunk tank. It was my idea. Our attorney refused to believe she might be lying about how many days she was in rehabilitation. I insisted we subpoena the records to prove she couldn't make it through the program. She only lasted three days. The remaining 27 were spent on the beach getting a tan. Her parents enabled her to pull this ruse by paying for her to stay at a hotel for 27 days. The records revealed all her feelings and her chemical problems.

In conclusion, I exposed the alcohol problem with a three-pronged attack: surveillance at lunch, wine bottles in the trash, and solid witness statements. Plus I exposed how wrong professionals can be. The psychologist failed to diagnose Doris and our own attorney underestimated his opponent. The subpoenaed records sealed the deal.

In this case, it was the nanny who confirmed Doris would rather store wine than groceries. The interview with the nanny painted a dismal picture of an alcoholic mother with no parenting skills as well as an evil person who sought revenge. As the facts unraveled, so did the true personality of Doris.

Doris is a person unlikely to share her children with the father. People need to know what's important to prove in the child custody community. Doris neglected the children by not buying food. She did not provide diapers or formula when Doris took the children to pre-school. Doris never picked them up on time. Doris drank and drove with the children in the car. She left the baby in the bathtub alone. She let the toddler play next to a loaded gun. The children had no regimen. Doris was incapable of providing the basics of childcare. Children can't grow and be healthy in this kind of chaos.

I couldn't have asked for a more damaging interview than the nanny. The psychologist admitted defeat. He knew now Doris was a liar and a drunk.

Although the psychologist didn't like Bob, he recommended sole custody to him with minimum visitation for Doris until she's able to prove she is alcohol-free!

Impeaching the Court-Appointed Psychologists

The use of experts in custody cases must be addressed because more and more experts are used in many different ways. Typically forensics psychologists are appointed in custody cases to perform a family study. As I have said throughout the book, the court-appointed psychologist generally makes a recommendation to the judge or court where the children will reside or what the custody arrangement will be. But what do you do when the psychologist doesn't render a favorable report for your family study? This is where your attorney can show their lawyering skills—or they may run and hide. Attorneys don't like to rock the boat with psychologists because they will see them again on another case. The only problem with this scenario is you have to live with the results of an unfavorable evaluation by the forensic psychologists.

In my opinion, what separates a good attorney from a bad attorney in custody disputes is the ability to overcome an unfavorable evaluation by a psychologist. Now some of the time parents deserve an unfavorable evaluation. When this happens, there's not a lot an attorney can do to repair their case. On the other hand I have seen a lot of unfavorable evaluations in custody disputes that were undeserving. I will upset the legal community with this comment, but most attorneys don't have the intestinal fortitude to challenge an unfavorable evaluation. Unfortunately, this is where your expensive attorney fails you.

I have parents tell me they didn't need an attorney in their case because after they received an unfavorable evaluation their case was over anyway. Yet they paid their attorney thousands of dollars to receive what? Too many attorneys let the psychologists determine the fate of your child. Psychologists bring their own biases to these family studies or psychological evaluations. Because of this they are not impartial by any means.

The first thing you need to impeach the erroneous evaluation is an attorney who has the guts to try. Most attorneys won't rock the boat, and they have a hundred excuses for not challenging the psychologist. Of course the biggest excuse is confrontation. Most attorneys just don't want to confront another professional for their incompetence. The psychological community is small and most attorneys don't want the reputation of spanking psychologists when they misbehave.

In the hundreds of custody cases I have reviewed, I find it almost easy to poke holes in most psychological evaluations because most evaluations are incomplete anyway. Generally they consist of a psychological exam and a few interviews. Just like attorneys and judges, psychologists are overworked, and they confuse and mix up their cases. But the evaluation is just simply incomplete to decide the future of a child. The following steps can help prove an erroneous evaluation:

- Interview witnesses and character witnesses.
- Subpoena the psychologist's notes in your evaluation.
- Depose the court-appointed psychologist.
- Hire another psychologist to critique your erroneous evaluation.

Typically during a family study, the psychologist will ask you for names of character witnesses, teachers, or friends who have watched you interact with the child. It's been my experience that half the time the psychologists don't even contact these people to see if they have any positive or negative experiences with you, or they will contact a disproportionate amount of people. For example, they might contact three of your witnesses and 10 of your spouse's witnesses. If this is the case, this needs to be made an issue in your evaluation. Not only is it disproportionate, but it is also incomplete.

The other issue might be whether or not the witnesses are biased. I have seen psychologists interview only family members for one spouse and only teachers, babysitters, or principals for the other. Obviously, the biased parties are going to have mostly positive comments about their family. Occasionally, I have interviewed family members who have turned on their family for one reason or another, and this can be helpful in custody battles. Also, I have interviewed witnesses to prove the psychologist did not interview them.

I have found that subpoenaing the psychologist's notes is very helpful because in most cases the psychologist files a written report or evaluation of the family study. I have found on many occasions the notes psychologists take during their evaluation don't reflect or are not consistent with their report. This is where you have a truly erroneous report, because the psychologist for whatever reason snubbed you. They sabotaged your evaluation.

Of course this is despicable, but it happens. And of course you can file a complaint with the court or psychology board but first you need to reverse the damage. This kind of sabotage is where the psychologist loses credibility. This gives you options in your case that your attorney will need to craft to maximize the impact.

At this point you may want to depose the psychologist to point out the erroneous report. This will take careful preparation. Your attorney may need to hire a forensic psychologist to consult on how to pigeonhole the court-appointed psychologist who sabotaged your case. The new expert you hire may break your case wide open.

The expert may be able to critique the erroneous report and compare it to the notes you subpoenaed to show the inconsistencies. They may craft questions for your attorney to ask at the deposition or evaluate the psychological tests you took to determine if the tests are consistent with the report or notes. Your expert may find problems with all of these variables. If necessary, your expert may need to testify against your court-appointed psychologist to impeach their evaluation. The order of how you attack the evaluation is something you will need to address with your expert and your attorney. I have seen judges throw the erroneous evaluation back at the psychologist and tell them to start over. But I caution you that it is rare for a psychologist to change their evaluation. They don't like to be wrong or proven wrong.

Another issue in this evaluation is the discovery, depositions, or any investigation that was done in your case prior to the family study. If your attorney submitted evidence about your spouse that the court-appointed psychologist ignored, you can use this information as the basis to impeach them. Often, psychologists ignore some information and focus on other issues that aren't relevant. So it is arbitrary, or just one opinion stacked against another. For example some psychologists in custody disputes don't care if the parents have sleepovers in front of the child, where another will think it is taboo. Some judges may think it is reasonable behavior while others think it has a catastrophic impact on the child. So unfortunately there are no absolutes in custody. That's why careful preparation is so important. Using experts in your case may be necessary to reverse a bad or erroneous evaluation. You may need other experts to help you in your case. Other types of experts include:

- Child psychologists
- Child psychiatrists
- Pediatricians

Child psychologists are concerned with development of the mental and behavioral processes from birth to maturity. The child psychologist may have many applications in custody cases. One, the child psychologist may treat the child for any behavioral problems that stem from the trauma of divorce. The child may have a chemical imbalance and need to be treated by a medical doctor such as a child psychiatrist. Sometimes, the court will appoint a child psychologist in addition to a psychologist to perform a study of the family during a custody battle. This usually happens when the family has had a death in the family or a trauma that may need a specialist in child psychology.

Pediatricians are medical doctors who specialize in diseases and ill-nesses in children. The application of a pediatrician for custody may be to prove that a parent is either molesting the child or abusing the child. In cases I have seen, the pediatrician may testify to bruises, beatings, or evidence of molestation.

The disturbing application in custody is when a parent takes the child to a child psychologist who is not court-appointed for the purpose of alienating the other parent. An example would be that the custodial parent takes the child to a child psychologist and convinces the thera-pist that the child is having behavioral problems because of the other parent. The custodial parent attempts to brainwash the child by telling them they won't get to see each other anymore because the non-custo-dial parent is taking them away. This kind of manipulation damages the child, who may then withdraw from the non-custodial parent. The child psychologist may only see one side and may recommend custody to the custodial parent. I have seen cases where the therapist doesn't even meet with the non-custodial parent before making a recommen-dation.

You might think no therapist would be this stupid or incompetent, but think again! This tactic has become very common in custody bat-tles. The custodial parent usually has an advantage, depending on the law in your state, because they have legal control of the child.

The custodial parent can legally take the child to a therapist where in many cases—depending on the law—the non-custodial parent cannot take the child to a therapist without the consent of the court. The cus-todial parent uses the expert as a weapon to alienate the non-custodial parent. If the court appoints a child psychologist to evaluate the child, at least the non-custodial parent has the eyes of the court to monitor the conduct of the child psychologist. In this example, the child psy-chologist may detect that the custodial parent may be alienating the other parent. Simply put, the custodial parent may be the reason the child is having behavioral problems, because the child resides with them. Because the custodial parent has more access to the child, the child psychologist may reach this conclusion.

If a parent is manipulating an expert, your attorney should either hire another expert or depose the expert to refute their findings. If both parents are not included in the therapy of the child, this may be reason to refute the expert's finding. Both parents still have rights, which the expert should adhere to.

Today, because of specialization, there are all kinds of experts, including experts on sexual addiction, chemical dependency, sexual abuse, forensics, and security.

Child Molestation

Whether the charge of child molestation is fact or fiction, the damage is done to the entire family. In some states, for example, if a mother accuses a father of child molestation, the government or Child Protection Services (CPS) will most likely investigate the claim. The problem is even if it is a prank, it becomes an effective tactic for preventing visitation by the accused parent.

During a divorce, accusations of child molestation are rarely true. It's often used as a weapon against the other parent to thwart visitation, thus cutting off the bond between parent and child. But if we look at the psychology of this tactic or claim, in many cases it backfires on the accuser. I have seen psychologists view this as a sick and demented tactic and reverse custody almost instantly. Many psychologists believe that any parent willing to frivolously file molestation charges is capable of almost anything. Another uphill battle for the accuser is proving molestation. I have seen cases where penetration has been proved on an infant girl. Now you have the problem of whodunit. Were they in the care of the mother or the father at the time of penetration? And how can you prove when it was perpetrated? The other problem is the government might take the child away based on the allegation that molestation took place. So both parents can lose in this scenario. It is more common for fathers to be accused of molestation than mothers. It is also a fact that child molesters are generally men instead of women. Accurate statistics are not available, but according to social workers and police officers I have interviewed, the majority of the child molestation charges filed during a divorce are frivolous.

I asked myself why Mia Farrow waited until her nasty divorce to file child molestation charges on Woody Allen. I mean, if Woody Allen molested any of the children and Mia knew about it, why didn't she speak up earlier? I have seen psychologists flip on custody because of this very issue. One of the parents is so obsessed with the children that they accuse the other parent of child molestation. And to complicate matters further, they have the children examined by a pediatrician as well as a child psychologist and put the children through a perverse ordeal because they are actually ill themselves. Their obsessive-compulsive behavior is destructive to the family.

That's why I say to my clients if you accuse a parent of molestation, you better be able to prove you're right. In my many years as a private investigator I have installed cameras in businesses for the purpose of theft control, etc. Now we have entered a new era of installing cameras in homes to prove parents are lewd and perverse or the babysitter beats their children. Welcome to the 21st century, where parents install cameras in bathrooms to see if one of the parents is actually molesting the children while they bathe.

Molestation must be proved! This is a sensitive issue that could be destructive to the family for many years to come. These are at least some of the steps to take if you suspect molestation:

1. You must isolate the child and who was with the child.

2. You must seek professional help with doctors who specialize in abuse and molestation.

3. You must take pictures or video of the injury.

4. You must report the abuse to the police.

If you are going to take pictures of bruises or any body part of a child, you should have a witness present. One of the points I have tried to make in this book is that you need an unbiased party when you gather evidence. You never want to be in the position of accusing without proof. You need witnesses for everything you do. As far as video is concerned, you don't necessarily need witnesses because you can see the action before, during, and after. From a creative point of view, there are ways of customizing a video package to meet your needs. The technology is improving all the time for size and clarity. So don't assume you can't video a room because of the design.

One final note about child molestation: Naturally if it is true a child is being molested, it's something you want to stop immediately. However—and this is true in child custody a lot of the time—you have to prove damage to prevent damage. You need to give enough rope to the parent to hang themselves. The fact a parent is mentally ill may not be enough. So whether it is neglect, abuse, or molestation, generally you will need to prove these factors to secure your children.

According to the Center Against Sexual Abuse, here are some signs to look for regarding abuse:

- Unusual interest or knowledge of sex acts or language inappropriate for the child's age.

- Seductive behavior with adults or children.

- Excessive masturbation.

- Wearing layers of clothing regardless of weather.

- Reluctance to go to a particular place or to be with a particular person.

- Compulsive behavior, such as constant washing.

- Abrupt change in behavior or personality.

- Withdrawal, depression, excessive crying.

- Inappropriate dress, such as tight and/or revealing clothing.

- Marked decline in school.

- Suicidal threats, risky behaviors, self-mutilation.

- Marked reaction to sex education at school.

- Avoidance of bathroom. Often, sexual abuse takes place in bathrooms.

These are common behavior characteristics of children who have been sexually abused. Any one of these characteristics may not indicate abuse.

IX COMMANDMENT
PROVE YOUR CASE

Once you have all the evidence and your case is prepared, you have to prove your case. This means all parties and participants in this case need to be aware of the evidence and issues that will decide your custody battle. The psychologist should have your evidence, and often you will need to go to court to make the judge aware of your evidence. Even if your case doesn't go to trial, the judge needs to see your evidence because *this is never over.*

V

Investigation

How to Use an Investigator

This book is about how to gather evidence in child custody cases, which is exactly what an investigator should be doing in your case. I believe in investigation by objective, just like management by objective. But few people understand what can be investigated in custody cases. Lifestyle is one of the most important aspects of a child custody case. Throughout this book I have talked about lifestyle or personality types. Investigators can essentially document a given lifestyle, whether they use photographs, videotape, or eyewitness testimony.

What few people understand is what is considered a lifestyle. For example, you may hire an investigator and videotape a parent driving around drunk with the children in the car. If this is a lifestyle, it needs to be documented on several occasions. You can't just catch a parent one time. You must catch the parent at least a few times in behavior that is not in the best interest of a child. And there are many ways to do that.

In "The Case of the Doctor's House Call," I employed several investigative tools to prove my case. I used eyewitness testimony by following my subject to lunch and watching her drink. I used the trash audit by going through her trash and finding plenty of wine bottles. I also videotaped her picking up her children from childcare after she had downed several drinks. I employed more than one tactic to prove this woman had an alcohol problem.

As a client, you must stay open minded that more than one tactic can be used to prove a parent is unfit. The fire you build should be built as big as possible. So overkill is really not an issue. The only time over-kill is a consideration is when you risk getting caught. In other words, you don't want to put your investigator at risk of getting caught if it isn't necessary. You might want to save the investigator to employ at a more useful time. I tell my clients this especially when it involves inter-viewing. Because once you unleash the investigator to interview a wit-ness, your opponent will know you have hired an investigator. So *when* you investigate is as important as *how* you investigate.

One of the biggest complaints among investigators is that attorneys don't know how to use them effectively. They use them usually when it is too late. Or they just don't know or understand the investigator's capabilities. For example the best time to employ an investigator is before you even get an attorney. Chances are the attorney will screw it up. Attorneys often attempt to win their cases through legal gymnastics instead of carefully gathering evidence.

If an attorney is going to attempt to gather evidence in a custody case, they will most likely use subpoena power. This is necessary in most cases, but timing is important. As I've already said several times, surprise attack is usually the best course of action to document a life-style. If you hire an attorney before you hire an investigator, chances are the attorney will lose the element of surprise. A lot of attorneys just don't think in tactical terms.

Most attorneys don't hire investigators for two reasons. First, the attorney just doesn't understand what an investigator can do for them. They are not investigators so they don't fully appreciate what we do. Second, attorneys don't want to share fees. They know there is only so much money to go around in a case, and they want it all.

I want to change the way you view your custody case. Most people just hire an attorney and hope they take care of it. This is the biggest mistake you can make. If you leave everything to your attorney, you're destined for big trouble. You must get involved in your own case. So take the lead and if it is necessary to hire an investigator, hire one. Don't wait for your attorney to sabotage your case first by filing motions and subpoenas. This will only warn your opponent.

How to Choose an Investigator

Follow these steps to find the investigator that's right for you:

1. Call the best family attorneys and get their referral.

2. Call friends and associates for a referral.

3. Interview the investigator for their experience.

4. Ask the investigator for referrals, and call them.

If you need to prove a lifestyle, you need to hire a good investigator. Of course the next hurdle is how to find a good investigator. This becomes a mission in itself. I would call the best attorneys in town and ask them who they use. I would contact other people who have gone through a nasty custody battle and see who they hired. The last thing you want to do is use the yellow pages. The investigators in the yellow pages are the investigators who don't usually have a referral system. Some of them do bad work so they depend on their big ads to get them work. But most people believe in brand names or they believe the investigator with the largest ad must be good. These are the people who call me up after they have been ripped off and want me to clean up the mess. The only problem is they don't have any money left.

It takes some effort to find a good investigator, attorney, gardener, or any other type of business. Because you are reading this book you are miles ahead in your case. My hope is that not only are you learning about custody but that you're also learning ways to avoid getting ripped off. This book familiarizes people with investigative techniques. So when you do hire an investigator, you can tell them what you want and know a little about how it can be accomplished. You need to interview the investigator like you would for any service. You need to see the investigator face to face and judge their appearance. You want to know their background and experience. And even if they don't understand custody issues, you might still want to hire them if they are skilled in the techniques of gathering evidence, such as interviewing witnesses, surveillance, and document retrieval.

Chances are you are not going to find an investigator who has fought their own custody battle. So they may not have the knowledge that you would like for your case. They may be good investigators, but they just don't have the specialized knowledge in custody. That's okay because you need to direct their efforts anyway. Nobody knows your case like you do. So the investigator can still interview or establish a lifestyle in your case. Good investigators have the following characteristics:

1. They are good listeners.

2. They are analytical.

3. They have a good appearance.

4. They have good manners.

Investigators have to be good listeners so they can fully understand the situation and respond. Details are very important in custody cases. If the investigator doesn't listen, they will miss an important detail that could later hurt the case. This is my complaint with attorneys. A lot of attorneys are so arrogant they fail to listen to their clients. Consequently, they fail to maximize their abilities in a given case.

Investigators need to be analytical. But investigators need to know who to investigate or interview first and what kind of approach they are going to take in a given case.

Investigators need a good appearance. What I mean is investigators need to have a professional appearance. For example, you might want to take your investigator with you to meet your attorney. If you want to impress upon your attorney how good or how necessary your investigator is to your case, appearance is important. By the same token, when you unleash your investigator to interview people, they will get better results if they are clean-cut and professional looking.

It's more difficult to be contemptible to somebody when they are polite. I have seen investigators spend more time trying to intimidate witnesses instead of communicate. Sometimes witness intimidation is necessary, but I have found people to cooperate more when I have been polite.

An investigator can be the middleman between success and failure. The investigation can build and win your case. Unfortunately, investigation has taken a back seat in civil and domestic cases for quite some time. This makes no sense to me when you consider that investigation is the backbone of criminal law, where the burden of proof is more extreme than in civil cases. Yet in custody cases, proof is also important when you consider how difficult it is to prove a parent is unfit. This is even more of a reason to employ investigators in custody cases. Investigators can prove lifestyle, personality problems, neglect, jeopardy, alcoholism, drug abuse, infidelity, and child abuse. How investigators prove this can be accomplished in a variety of ways. Don't assume something can't be proven because you tried and failed. The trained investigator can prove many things using many techniques.

Interviewing

The importance of interviewing cannot be underestimated. Eyewitness testimony (such as a neighbor who witnesses a crime) is worth its weight in gold. Eyewitness testimony is extremely important and a credible part of a criminal case. The same applies in child custody. What the neighbor or co-worker witnesses may be the deciding factor in a given case. I like to win my cases through interviewing. Yes, the cloak and dagger stuff sounds good and sometimes it's necessary. But good interviews from credible witnesses can have a lot of impact and it's economical, too. Surveillance by the hour can be very expensive, but a few good interviews can turn your case for you.

Some witnesses are very cooperative, while some will tell you to pound dirt because they don't want to be involved. That's when I go through my advanced salesmanship routine. I make people feel guilty for not talking to me. For example my job is very negative. People don't call me because they are getting married or baptized or having a baby. They call me because they have a problem. My job is to solve the problem.

I explain to the witness that people are in jail unjustly because witnesses didn't come forward and tell the truth. There are witnesses who watched a hit and run where people have been killed and they don't come forward. Then I put this on the witness by telling them it could happen to them or somebody in their family. Some difficult people can be turned around. I have even been skillful enough to create empathy and sympathy for me for just doing my job.

Interviewing is so overlooked in custody cases. In the "Diary" section, I talk about the importance of a diary as an interviewing tool for the lawyer, psychologist, and investigator. The application may vary, but the impact may make the difference in your case. Also the diary attempts to persuade or ensure that the psychologist does their job. Sometimes the psychologist will ask a parent for a list of teachers, childcare workers, or character witnesses to interview. I believe this is well intended by the psychologist in your case. But half the time they never get around to interviewing these people. Consequently, they fail to perform their job in my opinion. For example, if a teacher spends the most time with a child, then it would make sense to interview the child's teachers.

Teachers spend six hours a day five days a week with children. Parents only have the ability to spend a couple of hours a day five days a week with their children. In many cases, teachers bond with the children. Through this process they are able to determine problems the child may have at home.

In these cases, it's to your advantage to have a psychologist interview teachers or childcare workers. If the psychologist is court-appointed, they have a better chance of receiving cooperation. But if the psychologist is not doing their job, you must ensure the facts are collected and utilized.

I didn't write this book to bash lawyers, judges, and psychologists. I wrote this book to help people. But because the system is controlled and saturated with these professionals, I have no choice but to point out the shortcomings.

Interviewing is important but so is who you interview and how you interview them. There are basically two types of interviews. The field interview is a face-to-face interview. Some witnesses or potential witnesses will avoid face-to-face interviews because they are perceived as confrontational. Because most people try to avoid confrontation, these interviews may have to be over the phone.

The advantage of face-to-face interviews is that people tend to loosen up when they get comfortable. If the interviewer is good, they may get a lot more information that way. On the other hand, telephone interviews may be easier for some witnesses and they may gab on the phone all night long. But either way, you need to document the conversation. If tape recording is illegal in your state without consent, then you may have them sign a statement. The statement is essentially a signed account of what they witnessed.

Obviously, asking the right questions is important to the interview. This is where the relationship with the client, investigator, paralegal, or attorney is important. Nobody knows your case better than you do. So if a witness has intimate details about a lifestyle or bad parenting, these questions need to be structured. Simply rehearse the information before the interview.

Sometimes background information about the witness is essential. For example, if your spouse was previously married, you might want the investigator to talk to the ex-spouse about their experience during that marriage. This may shed light on their personality. If their experience was one of abuse, it may show a pattern of behavior. This is critical to the psychologist to evaluate the personality of the parent.

If the investigator is able to view the documents from a previous divorce case, criminal case, or civil action, it can paint a useful picture in your present case. The interview of a witness may reveal the parenting skills or personality type of a parent, so I focus on the children in an interview. That is, I ask the witness questions regarding a parent's interaction with their child. The parenting skills and the personality type should be put on trial.

Some states have no-fault divorce. So for the purposes of a divorce, the lifestyle is irrelevant. But when children are involved, the lifestyle becomes very important.

All neighbors have an opinion even if they don't want to express it. Unfortunately, a lot of investigators don't understand what's relevant in custody battles. But then, often "you" the client don't either. If one parent talks negative about the other in front of the children or in front of a witness, then we need to document this behavior. And of course there are numerous parents who cannot perform even the basics of childcare, such as cleanliness, naps, nutrition, and discipline. If these simple tasks are not maintained, it needs to be documented and should be a part of the interview.

Naturally if either parent is an alcoholic or drug addict, it needs to be covered in the interview. The neighbors may also be able to supply you with babysitters' names or they may have babysat themselves. If so, you need to document how often they're with the children.

Neglect is an issue. Why have custody if you don't spend time with the children? But as you know, children become a possession in custody cases. Playing "keep away" or denying visitation is a common practice. If a witness has knowledge of this, the investigator needs to record it for court purposes.

The equation has two parts: bad parenting and personality type. You may have no idea what your spouse has said to other people about you or your children. The witness may lead you to yet another witness who will help your case. For example, what if your spouse told one of your friends they had an affair when they were in Aspen on the Fourth of July when they were supposed to be at Disneyland. Secondly, what were they doing and who were the players? Obviously somebody is lying.

Building the personality type can be accomplished through interviews. In my opinion, women make the best witnesses. The reason is because most women know good parenting skills even if they don't possess them. They tend to judge other mothers critically. Also, women pay attention to detail. For example, women will notice immediately if a mother is ignoring one child and favoring another. Women can even tell you what the mother is wearing from head to toe. Women notice body language on other women as well. By considering a typical day in the life of your child or spouse, you can determine the people they come in contact with who might make good witnesses.

Some people are just evil, diabolical, or mentally ill. If this is the case, it needs to be pointed out. That's why I said earlier that you must change the way you think about your spouse if you want custody. If you focus on the pain and anger, you won't win the case. But if you focus on what's best for your child, your chances of winning improve. Unfortunately some parents have no business raising children because they just don't have the instincts, patience, or personality to lead their children into a positive and meaningful life.

For the purposes of interviewing, you need to make a checklist of witnesses, then arrange the order you interview them to maximize your impact. For example, you would want to interview former babysitters before you interview present ones. That way, you can prevent the witnesses from being tampered with. Once the investigation is launched or interviews are conducted, the opposition may try to tamper with the witnesses or prevent them from talking.

By the same token, when a witness is willing to talk, get it while it's hot. Months later the witnesses may be reluctant to go to court, so you want to lock them in early and record the interview to use later in case they change their minds.

Once the word is out that an investigation has begun, don't be afraid to interview biased family members, including grandparents, uncles, aunts, sisters, brothers, or anyone else—even if you perceive they are the enemy. I have interviewed people who you would never believe would talk and they have. Once they fear they may have to testify in court, they usually talk or they may completely avoid the situation. But either way they have a problem. If they don't cooperate, that's good information, too, because it shows their lack of interest in their own family. If they talk and tell the truth, they may turn on their own family members. This scenario is actually common. That's why timing is important. Some family members may be reluctant to speak with an investigator. But the psychologist is court-appointed and wields a lot of power, so they may have some success getting family members to cooperate.

Techniques of Surveillance

As I write this book, I continually think tactically as to what is really relevant and what isn't. Some private investigators will smash a bug with a hammer if you let them. In other words, they will investigate unnecessarily. Surveillance is one of the most expensive and difficult aspects of investigation, and investigators get burned every day because they are not alert or trained to sneak and peek. I break down surveillance into three types:

1. Pointing

2. Front tails

3. Team

Pointing

I worked a custody case that had already been worked. The client warned me that the last investigator, an ex-cop, got caught in the first 15 minutes. Some former police officers make good investigators, but some of them were only patrol officers and surveillance is not their forte. I hope they don't train at your expense. Fortunately on this case I didn't get caught and my client won sole custody. The mother was tagged with supervised visitation.

The reason the investigator was caught was because he sat outside the home waiting for the subject to leave. Wrong move! In Arizona the homes are generally close together and conspicuous vehicles stick out like a yellow cab. So I invented the concept of **pointing**, in which you watch your subject from a point of access control. An example would be to locate the exits to a given area, then set up your surveillance there. That way the subject has to pass by sooner or later when they leave.

The other principle of pointing is to wait at some other location where the subject will appear; therefore minimizing the potential to be discovered. For example, let's say you know your spouse gets her hair cut every Friday at 9 a.m. at Susie's Hair Salon. The investigator goes to Susie's Hair Salon and follows the subject from there. Maybe your spouse exercises at the gym every Monday, Wednesday, and Friday at 5 p.m. The investigator would wait there and follows him after his workout. People are creatures of habit. Whether it is drugs, alcohol, or sex—people have routines, which need to be considered when determining the surveillance.

Caution: You must be alert because during surveillance nothing happens for hours and then all hell breaks loose and you are on your way at a moment's notice.

Generally people who are concerned about being followed have something to hide. They may drive in circles for a few minutes to shake the investigator. But if you meet them at their planned destination and follow them from there, they often don't suspect they will be followed from that location.

What Is the Importance of Pointing?

Pointing can be very important in extreme cases, such as heavy drug or alcohol use, or criminal behavior. People allege all types of behavior regarding their spouses when they want custody, but proving it is another matter. Sometimes the only way to prove behavior is through surveillance. I was fortunate in the situation where the ex-cop was caught during the first fifteen minutes of surveillance. This happened because the client lost the element of surprise. But in some extreme cases, the behavior is so addictive they can't change their behavior and ultimately the truth will surface.

Front Tail

Another technique of surveillance is the **front tail** or following from the front. I'm sure I didn't invent this technique, but in some situations it can work. Paranoid people are constantly looking back rather than in front for a tail. This technique takes real skill and I generally don't recommend this to amateurs. However, I have years of experience and this technique has served me well many times.

Team Surveillance

Pointing and front tail are options when you are surveilling with man-on-man coverage. It can and should be used when you have the resources to employ **team surveillance.**

Team surveillance is the most expensive technique of surveillance. This technique is more common with government agencies because they have the resources. Essentially, two or more vehicles are used to follow the subject. If watching, the subject will probably fail to determine if they are being followed because the team will rotate vehicles or investigators while using radios to communicate the rotation. Remember, if you think I am behind you, I am probably ahead of you!

Tapes

I recommend to all my clients taping. The importance of taping cannot be underestimated. But caution: some states don't allow it. In Arizona it's perfectly legal to tape a conversation with someone without their permission as long as you are involved in the conversation. But in some states it's a crime to tape conversations even if you are participating.

There are several ways of using a tape in custody battles. Often the psychologist determines custody, so if necessary give the tapes to the court-appointed psychologist. Remember of course that the conversation exploits both Parents' problems. It's amazing what people say to each other. I remember a client I had and I told him to record the mother because she threatened him all the time. She thought because he was on his car phone that he couldn't tape her, but because of hands-free phone systems he would just turn on his tape and record. She told him that when her son was old enough, she was going to tell him he is a bastard and that the father was a drug dealer. What a nice person she was!

A taped conversation helps build the personality type for the psychologist. If a parent is denying visitation, taping their conversations can often prove it. Sometimes people have sudden surges of anger similar to a seizure. This may be a person with an illness who is more easily identified by a psychologist if they have the tapes.

Another important element of taping is lying. You can easily prove a liar with tapes. Again this helps the psychologist identify any personality problems a parent may have. In another case I worked, a grandmother told me her daughter was threatening to murder her children like Susan Smith. I told her to tape that conversation so she could convince the police it was a legitimate concern. I said if you call the police without taping the threats, they will not act on it and neither will the courts. I went to the grandmother's home to set up the tape and she ultimately recorded her daughter threatening to murder her grandchildren. My client then called an attorney who asked for an emergency hearing for change of custody. The police went out and took the children away from the ill mother and placed the children temporarily with the grandparents.

Admissibility

Psychologists are not concerned with admissibility. If they are performing the custody evaluation, your case may be won before you go to court. The object is to win before you go to court, which can prevent more costs later. I recommend that you label the tapes and dictate on the tape the date and time. If you don't have a court-appointed psychologist in your case and you are taping your conversations, you should consult an attorney for admissibility in your state. However, a lot of attorneys don't understand evidence and its preparation or admissibility, so do your homework on this issue.

Other Tapes

If you hire a private investigator for your case to interview witnesses, the investigator must tape record the interviews. You must lock them in early because people change their minds about testifying. People love to talk but not in a courtroom.

In a case I worked on, the babysitter filed police reports attempting to get my client arrested for visitational interference. Later when we subpoenaed the long distance bill, we saw the mother had called the police on my client from another state and reported that my client never brought the child back. Well my client was not going to leave a one-year-old baby on the doorstep in temperatures approaching 110 degrees. The fact was, my client took the baby back on time but nobody was home. The mother called the police long distance and then called the babysitter and told her to get over to the house and tell the police the father hadn't returned the child.

Later I asked the babysitter to admit on tape that she lied to the police. This happened three times and three times false police reports were filed. The babysitter was locked into her story on tape and ultimately explained to the court how she lied to the police for the mother. This gets even better because I thought the mother would be upset when we subpoenaed the babysitter to court. So I told the attorney to ask the babysitter if the mother threatened her life if she testified. Guess what the answer was?

Film

A picture paints a thousand words. In custody cases, film (photographs and/or videotape) may be testimony to the strange things people do with their lives. I have filmed clothes thrown in the trash because the wife was upset at her husband, and backyards with swimming pools that have no fence around them. I have filmed children in cars without a car seat, a two-year old riding on the front seat of a motorcycle at fifty miles per hour, hobos sleeping in the front yard of a home, fathers driving drunk with their children in the car, and mothers driving around with suspended licenses.

And of course I have filmed people committing adultery. In a no-fault divorce state, adultery isn't an issue in divorce. But in child custody cases it can be! Who somebody is fornicating with is important when it comes to pointing out the personality type of the mother or father. Some people have no guilt for the things they do. Ironically, some people who can't bond with their spouses also have trouble bonding with their children. Furthermore, catching adulterers on film may prove lies. And lies are important to psychologists.

Capturing key moments on film can make a real difference in your case. For example, if a mother is bringing in multiple partners in the house, it's a custody issue. Filming the episode with the date along with a timestamp can shed some real light on the truth.

Night photography is difficult and I recommend video for evening surveillance. However, if people go into a well-lit restaurant, the investigator may succeed in getting a good picture. You need different cameras for different jobs. If light is an issue, I recommend a specialist.

Some children are exposed to nude men walking around the house. Children should not be exposed to nude men at all; but especially a strange man their mother just picked up in a nightclub. Some women or men are addicted to sex or relationships. If this is true, this personality flaw needs to be exposed. Sometimes filming is the only way to point out behaviors and lifestyles. Film proves lies. It may prove alcohol or drug abuse, too. In "The Case of the Doctor's House Call," I photographed the wine bottles I fished out of the trash to show the mother was lying about her drinking.

On occasion, children are physically or sexually abused. This abuse may be preserved on film as evidence. However, in this situation you should have an unbiased party present when you film it so you cannot be accused of altering the injuries.

Film may prove the following:

1. Lies

2. Alcohol and drug abuse

3. Child abuse and sexual abuse

4. Lifestyle

5. Neglect and alienation

6. Criminal activity

Remember the psychologist may be able to make a more accurate recommendation to the court based on the evidence obtained. And sometimes the film as part of the investigation may push the psychologist over the edge to make a decision to determine custody.

Trash Audit

This subject has been written about before. But going through the trash is such an important tool in an investigation that it must be recognized. Everybody does it! I mean the FBI, the CIA, and me. Going through trash may give credence to the saying "you are what you eat." I am amazed at what people eat. Some parents will feed their children anything. But generally when I go through trash in custody cases I am looking for drugs or alcohol. I know what you're thinking—it's too easy. People would be more careful than that. They wouldn't throw out paraphernalia or roaches or bongs or beer cans or vodka bottles. Wrong. If somebody is a real alcoholic or drug addict, they don't know what they are doing half the time anyway. It's rare that they save their trash and throw it in back of their car and drive five blocks down the street to dispose of it.

I worked on a case when my client went to the "Wall Street Journal" and told them I had gone through the trash of some wealthy businessmen. The story was on the front page of the "Wall Street Journal" that a private investigator in Scottsdale, Arizona had gone through their trash. My client was in litigation with the businessmen and wanted to intimidate them.

My client thought we would never be able to go through their trash again, but I assured him that they would get tired of shredding the volumes of documents they assimilated. Sure enough, 60 days later I was sorting through their trash again.

How Is Trash Used?

I've used trash in all types of cases. But in custody cases I bag and tag beer cans or any alcoholic beverage bottle. I date it and I use gloves because fingerprints may be an issue. Yes it is true! If I don't see somebody drinking, I can go through their trash and still prove they are alcoholics. If they are the only adult living at the residence and I scoop the trash on a regular basis, who else would be drinking? Also I find receipts where they buy the alcohol. In one case I found the receipts and discovered the person had a habit of a liter of vodka every other day. I showed a picture of the woman to the liquor department in a grocery store and they identified my subject. She came in about four days a week and bought a liter of vodka.

The court-appointed psychologist will read the report of the investigator when they recommend custody. Trash can win your case. Trash identifies what movies a subject rents, what they eat and drink, and practically everything they do. There is mail, report cards, love letters, you name it—it gets thrown away.

If drugs or paraphernalia are found in the trash, the articles need to be examined by a forensic expert. There are law enforcement labs as well as private labs that will examine the evidence. If the parent you're investigating has a history of alcohol or drug abuse, this analysis may push your case over the edge. The judge may demand drug testing for the parent in question.

A trash audit is not always an option in custody cases. Sometimes people live in apartments, making it difficult to audit. If trash is not an option, then surveillance may be the alternative to prove drug and alcohol abuse.

Trash Audits: When and Who?

The important thing is to get the evidence you need for your case, and there's no time like the present. Of course, don't get caught because you will lose the element of surprise. Timing is always important in any investigation. But if a parent has an alcohol or drug problem, the trash usually will reveal it.

Only a licensed private investigator should go through the trash in your case. You need an unbiased person to investigate your case. If you personally went through the trash, you might be accused of planting the evidence. That's why several times in this book I have made the point that when possible have an unbiased person help with the field investigation of your case, where evidence needs to be collected.

VI

Other Issues

Accountability

We have talked about the system, its design, and how many things can go wrong. But what we haven't really addressed is accountability, including the judge, lawyers, parents, psychologist, and child.

Can you sue a judge? Can you sue a psychologist? Can you sue your lawyer? There are exemptions to whether you can sue a judge. This is something you would have to consult an attorney in your state to determine what your options are. However, even if the judge is exempt from an action involving the malfeasance of their decision in your case, there are options. Some states have a board that investigates judges, or you might want to hire somebody independent (or both). Some judges are corrupt just like anyone else. And if you can prove it or prove professionally unacceptable behavior, then you may get some kind of justice.

Typically the court-appointed psychologists are exempt from liability in custody cases. Again, you need to consult a good attorney to see what your recourse is, if any. But don't count it out. Sometimes psychologists are involved in people's lives prior to the divorce or the custody evaluation and they are not court-appointed. In the event they have damaged your family, you may have a case.

I remember a case when a mother was anticipating that her marriage was failing and she knew her husband would fight for equal time with the children. So she began taking them to a psychologist, but he wasn't specifically a child psychologist. Granted, one of the children had a slight learning disability. So it made sense for the child to get help. But probably the child needed a special teacher, not a psychologist.

The children saw the psychologist for three months before and during the divorce. During this time, the psychologist successfully destroyed the relationship the children had with their father. The psychologist was paid by the mother, which in my opinion made him biased. But the courts don't always see it that way. Also, the children didn't appear to have a very strong relationship with their father when the court-appointed psychologist tested them.

The so-called child psychologist manipulated the children for months before they were tested. This gave the mother plenty of time to plot and break down the family. Although the court-appointed psychologist awarded joint custody, the mother was awarded the children the majority of the time. As a result, the father had his children 40 percent of the parental time, but had no relationship with them because it had been undermined by the psychologist.

Does the father have recourse against the so-called child psychologist? Maybe, if damage to the children and relationship can be proved. But you would have to consult a good attorney case by case to see what the recourse is. I would recommend researching the complaints with the psychology board or licensing agent in your state. Locate as many people as you can who have a similar complaint or even a worse complaint and coordinate an effort to bar this psychologist from practicing. You might consider a class action suit, coupled by numerous complaints from people simultaneously to maximize the impact.

In my experience with licensing agents or the state bar for attorneys, they have been useless. I have filed complaints against attorneys and nothing gets done. However, to maximize the impact, you need to find other people who have sued or have been screwed by the psychologist to remove their license. If your goal is money, then consult an attorney. If you want the psychologist removed from practice, you might want to run an ad in the newspaper to attract other people who have been wronged and team up to fight this person. You might want to collect a legal fund for the project. There are options and you may want to exercise all of them.

Now attorneys who have committed "hari-kari" are another matter. Remember we have talked about accountability and the lack thereof. The fact is these attorneys work as many cases as they can. Few attorneys turn down cases in domestic relations, and the same is true for psychologists. And who knows how many cases the system has stuck judges with. As I have said before, I have watched psychologists confuse or forget their cases while testifying. I've seen attorneys forget to file motions, subpoena records, depose witnesses, etc. It's unbelievable. If the lawyer committed professional negligence, sue the bastard.

Unfortunately many lawyers are such sniveling worms it may be difficult to find one who has the stomach and courage to sue another one of their fraternity brothers and sisters. But to find a good lawyer, you need to interview attorneys and ask around to determine their quality of work. Again, if your goal is to yank the license of the attorney, you might want to take the steps I mentioned earlier about psychologists:

1. Locate other victims.

2. Check past and present complaints and lawsuits.

3. Run an ad in the newspaper to find more victims.

4. Start a legal fund for the battle that will ensue.

Again and again I have heard complaints that the domestic relations court is adversarial. Well of course it is. Many people who have either had to fight criminal or civil cases know this to be true. That's the justice system. And I don't think it will change for a long time. In our justice system, child custody is a game and if you don't know how to play, you will lose.

What Can Be Done?

The arrogance of the professionals today is they don't make mistakes. So if your attorney screws up or the psychologist screws up, they don't live with the mistakes, but you do. Your recourse in custody cases is difficult because you need professionals to design accountability for their own kind, though that may never happen. That's why one of the messages of this book is watch and monitor the professional in the system, and if necessary gather evidence on all parties. That's your chance to impact and account for the justice system. I eat, sleep, and drink custody cases every day, and there's no accountability for what I do. But I have a reputation to maintain, which means if I screw up one case, I might be out of business.

Professionals sabotage cases every day and live to tell about it. The wealthy attorney who messed up your case is still in business tomorrow working yet another one. The double standard that exists with attorneys is rather ridiculous. They view themselves as heroes. Yet they actually win or perform very rarely. This is the arrogance that goes along with being an attorney. Now if for some reason I didn't perform on a case, my name would be mud. Attorneys would ostracize me from their law practice.

Now that we know the system is flawed because of too many arrogant professionals, what can be done about accountability? In the short term it has to be you, the customer—and hopefully not the victim—who watches your rear. You have to insist that the people who comprise the system perform. If you have to send letters, send them. If

186

you have to fax reminders or storm into their offices, then do it. But self-reliance in the short term is the only hope for accountability in an overworked system. In the long term, accountability has potential, but like everything else in life, it takes work. I believe a legislative mandate limiting the case load for judges would slow down the machine and improve accountability. I believe the court should regulate custody evaluations, limiting the number of cases psychologists could have per month.

Attorneys probably can't be regulated because not all family attorneys practice only family law. Some of them practice criminal law and civil law. So trying to keep a handle on them would be an invasion of privacy. However, if the standards of professional liability for attorneys were upgraded, the market would take care of itself. And I base this only on the proposition that attorneys sue other attorneys.

And finally when a psychologist is appointed by the court, I believe an investigator should be appointed as well. I believe it would improve the accountability for many psychologists who never leave their offices.

The investigator can assist in an unbiased way by interviewing babysitters, neighbors, and teachers to cut to the truth. I know this controverts my position on using surprise attack in your investigation, but if you are going to expect the government to represent your best interest, this sacrifice needs to be made. While it's not a foolproof method, fewer cases will fall through the cracks when someone is in the field to seek the truth.

Parental Kidnapping

Parental kidnapping is one of the most traumatic events a parent can endure. The statistics are staggering. The legal quagmire it presents varies from state to state and country to country. If your child is kidnapped by a parent, you will need to involve every agency available to you, as well as child care workers, schools, neighbors, and employers.

There are many laws you will need to utilize to recover your child. The Uniform Child Custody Jurisdiction Act was formed to avoid controversy over what state has power to decide the outcome of jurisdictional conflict. Simply put, if the child has resided in a particular state for six consecutive months, the laws of that state have jurisdiction over the legal process and outcome of custody. The act was formed to provide stability to the home environment and deter abductions from state to state and to avoid more litigation of a custody dispute.

This act has many provisions depending on the custody order itself. In other words, depending on a given scenario, the rights of the parent when abduction occurs may differ depending on the existing custody order or agreement at the time of the abduction or if there is an order in place. If the parents are not divorced at the time of the abduction, the legal applications may differ from divorced parents because there is no court order in place at the time of the abduction.

Generally when abduction occurs, the parent who took the child is violating the law. However, the laws apply differently depending on the situation. This is why you must consult a qualified attorney who understands the Uniform Child Custody Jurisdiction Act, the Missing Child

Act, the Parental Kidnapping Prevention Act, and the International Child Abduction Remedies Act and how they apply to your situation.

The International Abduction Remedies Act applies to the provisions of the treaty called the Hague Convention. The Hague Convention, established in 1988, provides a venue for legal disputes in other countries. Not all countries are members of the Hague Convention. So if a child is abducted in the United States and is taken to a nonmember country, this may cause another legal quagmire for the recovery of the child. This doesn't mean the nonmember country won't cooperate—in some cases they might. But the members of the Hague Convention are required by international law to cooperate. The members' definition on cooperation may differ from country to country, so there are no absolutes regarding location and extradition of the abductor and the child.

Even if the law is on your side in a given case, it doesn't necessarily ensure cooperation in a timely fashion. I can tell you from experience that not all countries have extradition policies. In 1991, I assisted a parent recovering her children from Costa Rica, which at the time did not have an extradition policy. Recovering the children after we located them was simply a footrace from border to border. So your attorney and authorities will need to be consulted regarding the policies of the country in which your child was transferred. Because this is such a complicated situation, I am not going to burden you with all the legal scenarios because they may change from country to country on a yearly basis. The legislative process is continually changing regarding international abductions. However, I want you to be aware and informed that there are laws on the books in the United States and abroad that protect your rights.

What to Do when a Parental Kidnapping Occurs

Most parental kidnappings begin with visitational interference. This is the beginning of informing authorities that you are being denied your rights as a parent. If you can establish the child was kidnapped, then the FBI should be notified and the information should be entered in their National Crime Information Center (NCIC) computer. Your options when a child is abducted are:

1. Retain an attorney.

2. Report the abduction to the police.

3. Report the abduction to the FBI.

4. Report the abduction to the National Center for Missing & Exploited Children.

5. Hire a private investigator.

You need to retain a qualified attorney so you can understand and pursue the legal gymnastics of recovering your child. You need to report the abduction to the local police so they may assist you in locating your abducted child. Generally in big city police departments there are detectives who specialize in locating and recovering abducted children. If necessary, the local police will attempt to involve the FBI to help locate your child.

You need to inform the National Center for Missing & Exploited Children. This nonprofit organization is skilled in dispersing detailed information regarding the identity of your child, such as television, newspapers, etc.

You may need to retain the services of a qualified private investigator to aid in locating your child. Because government agencies are so overwhelmed with cases just like yours, often the trail may get cold by the time they attempt to locate your child. However, I suggest that you get in writing from the investigator what they can accomplish for you.

Methods of Locating Missing Children

There is no patent on locating children. You need to involve as many agencies as possible to locate a missing child. You may need to interview neighbors, employers, babysitters, relatives, childcare workers, or anyone who may have information. You may need a court order to subpoena school records, credit card companies, bank records, motor vehicle records, utility companies, or witnesses, depending on the situation.

You will need to carefully compile a checklist of investigative objectives to locate the missing child. This is why you need to enlist the services of attorneys, investigators, and government agencies to achieve a common goal.

Dealing with Stepparents

What role should stepparents play is a perplexing question among psychologists, lawyers, and judges. In my opinion, the stepparent's role should be limited during a custody battle because the opposition will accuse the stepparent of undermining the relationship between parent and child. The stepparent often becomes the object of scrutiny, and it's convenient to play the blame game with them. Often this is just an attempt to take the focus away from the real issues.

If this is your situation, you need to document this and use it against the parent who is attacking on these grounds. A diary can play a role in documenting this as well as interviewing witnesses who may substantiate any false allegations.

While the stepparent should play a limited role during the custody fight, that's not to say they should not work with the parent. They need to agree on what the rules are and still enforce them during the custody litigation. However, because added stress is put on the child during this period, the parenting needs to be handled with kid gloves. So you must pay extra attention to the emotional needs of the child during the litigation process.

If you do win custody, you also need to consider the adjustment for the children when they come to live with you, which could take several months. Remember, most children want to please both parents so that's why I have said you should never talk bad about the other parent in front of the child. In time, the child will recognize the problems their parent may have. So there is no need to bad-mouth the opposition. If the stepparent is fit, they might ultimately bond with the child.

Grandparents—the Emerging Client

According to the U.S. Census Bureau, approximately four million children live with their grandparents. Some of the reasons are because of divorce, death, drugs, or desertion. If you are a grandparent, you must consider whether you are up to the challenge of parenting a child at this stage of your life. Sometimes custody is not the answer, but going for custody is!

Winning custody may not be the result you want. But by going for custody, you might cause the parents to clean up their act. This doesn't always work and can be pretty expensive just to prove a point. But you may need to get an attorney and gear up for trial to provoke the parents to repair their lives.

Warfare is based on deception. You may not want to raise children at this stage of your life, but when you see your grandchild being abused or neglected, apathy is not the answer. Selfishness isn't either. I have seen grandparents fail to do anything in many extreme cases. I have also seen grandparents enable their own children by giving them money. Then the children abuse drugs and abuse their children, so the grandparents cut off their children and never see their grandchildren. Now the grandparents are in the situation of giving their children money just so they can see their grandchildren.

Grandparents have legal rights of visitation of their grandchildren. It is also true that if the children go up for adoption, the grandparents may lose their rights. Therefore, you will need to research the laws in your state.

If you're prepared for parenting as well as the task of suing and obtaining custody, good luck. The fact is custody is very possible for grandparents. On occasion, I have orchestrated an intervention where the grandparents got a counselor involved to try and shake out the truth about abuse going on among the parents and children. Sometimes it takes all the family members across the country to come in and pressure the parents into getting help so the children can be saved. Or maybe no family members are directly involved, but the intervention may still benefit the parents and the children in the long run.

Another option is guardianship. Essentially the parents sign the children over to the grandparents temporarily until they can get it together. With guardianship, you have physical and legal custody, usually for a six-month period. At the end of six months there may be a hearing to determine the progress of the people involved. Guardianship is ideal if parents just need financial assistance or they are cooperating with the grandparents to find a solution for their inability to parent.

Some grandparents are criticized for interfering in the raising of the grandchildren. I have had psychologists tell me grandparents spend their time spoiling their grandchildren instead of parenting them. They have also gone on to say the grandparents treat their adult children like children. Adults don't want their parents telling them how to raise kids, cook meals, and so on.

In these situations, the grandparents may be interfering. By the same token, in extreme cases where the parents are unfit or have a drug and alcohol problem, somebody needs to intervene and look out for the children. So grandparents walk a fine line between helping and controlling or interfering with the children. Of course, in a perfect world the parents should raise the children. I know from personal experience psychologists, attorneys, and CPS tend to side with the parents instead of the grandparents in many cases, even when the children may be at risk. Sometimes the psychologist will resent the grandparents for interfering, or they blame the grandparents for failing with their own children.

Their position could be now they are trying to control their children and grandchildren.

Before going for custody, grandparents need to know that:

1. It could be a long and expensive battle with no guarantees of winning.

2. They will need to *parent* instead of *grandparent* their grandchildren.

3. Regardless of whether they win or lose, the healing process will be slow with their own children.

4. They may only have the grandchildren temporarily.

5. They may be the only solution for the grandchildren.

The battle of custody can be a very expensive endeavor. A lot of grandparents are retired and on fixed incomes. Because of this, it may be a financial burden to battle for custody.

If the grandparents are going to be effective parents for their grandchildren, they are going to need to parent instead of grandparent. Children are natural manipulators and some grandparents depending on their age are not equipped to deal with children on a day-to-day basis.

When grandparents go to court and are legally awarded custody, it scars the relationship they had with their children. This scar may last forever.

The battle of a trial with witnesses testifying and assassinating their character can be awful. Even if the grandparents spend all the money and go to trial and win, the judge may reverse the decision if the parents improve or clean up their act. Therefore, custody could be temporary. But if this is so, the grandparents still in effect helped solve the problem.

The grandparents need to consider they may be the only solution to the children's welfare. The parents may never improve or clean up their act. So the grandparents need to mentally prepare themselves that they may have to raise the children. Unfortunately, this is often the case.

The parents may have serious drug or alcohol problems that are never cured, or the parents may end up in prison. Either way, the grandparents may be the only family members who can raise the children.

When grandparents petition for custody of their grandchildren, they are often faced with a dependency. A dependency is the juvenile court in your jurisdiction where your allegations will be heard by a judge. When the petition is filed, the judge will normally assign a caseworker from CPS to investigate the allegations in your petition to change custody. However, you as the grandparent don't have to petition for custody to file a dependency action. You may file a dependency action for the sole purpose of having the government investigate the parents for abuse or neglect.

However, if the government decides the parents are unfit and you don't want custody, then adoption may become the solution. Remember, if this happens, your rights as a grandparent may be terminated. As I said earlier, grandparents normally don't enjoy a warm reception from the court system. Of course there are exceptions, but generally grandparents have a lot of responsibilities and few rights legally.

If you are going to go for custody, investigation is even more important for grandparents. Because the court system is less tolerant of grandparents, your case better be prepared. Because a judge in the juvenile court most likely will hear your case, CPS will investigate the parents to see if they are fit. But they will also investigate the grandparents, because if you are potentially going to obtain custody of the children in question, it's their duty to know all parties and their parenting abilities.

Remember, the government can play dirty, and the focus of their investigation may be *you*, rather than the parents. Don't underestimate the government.

It's been my experience that CPS performs a substandard investigation. They are for the most part social workers not police detectives, though you may feel like they are police by their tone. They are often incompetent, but they have a lot of power. I have seen them defy court orders by the judge, suppress information regarding the background of the parents in question, and enable the parents in question. What CPS attempts to do in most cases is repair the family—even when it is not repairable. So they will coach the parents on how to beat the system.

These are the things you are up against as grandparents. That's why you need to investigate the parents thoroughly and independently from CPS. Because of the potential for CPS to turn on you, you need independent evidence of your claims against the parents. In fact, if your evidence is credibly gathered, you will embarrass CPS for their inability to expose the truth. This may be necessary for you to change custody of your grandchildren.

Social Programs

Because of the great expense for grandparents to assist in raising their grandchildren, there is federal government aid available in the form of child welfare. Aid to Families with Dependent Children (AFDC) may be an option for grandparents raising their grandchildren. Naturally there are guidelines for eligibility, which you'll need to research.

There may also be legal aid available to grandparents. This needs to be researched at the licensing board of attorneys at your state, county, and district. Some attorneys work pro-bono (free). Or sometimes-large law firms will donate a certain number of attorneys to work pro-bono each year for image and political reasons. The list of attorneys who work under these terms is usually posted with the state bar of your state.

The Case of Parental Termination

I watched Annie[1] and her son Tommy[2] for two years. Tommy's grandmother, Sherry[3], was my client. Sherry was an enabler. She gave Annie money and Annie drank it, smoked it, or snorted it.

One summer evening I was watching Annie's apartment, waiting for her to come home. It was a hot Arizona summer and I had bottled water but no food. I almost called for a pizza on my mobile phone and

---

1. Name has been changed to protect privacy
2. Name has been changed to protect privacy
3. Name has been changed to protect privacy

I would have had it delivered to my surveillance. But it was after 10 on a weeknight and a truck had just driven up in front of Annie's apartment, an old beat-up Chevy at least 10 years old with some dirtbag behind the wheel. This was the typical kind of guy Annie would consort with: long hair, unkempt, earring, tattoos.

Annie almost fell out of the truck. She had a quart bottle of beer in one hand and her son Tommy in the other. Tommy was about three and a half years old. Quickly I felt fear—fear for Tommy. Here's Annie drunk, holding her child, driving around with Joe Ragbag, who was probably drunk as a sailor himself. This is the kind of behavior that makes my teeth hurt. I wanted to rescue Tommy, shake Annie, and grab Joe Ragbag by his ponytail and buff-out the gray Bondo truck with his face.

Sherry hadn't really defined my mission. She was a typical mother/grandmother—the nice motherly type who could do detergent commercials. She grew up in the Midwest in a middle-class neighborhood. All her children were successes except Annie. Annie was an addict. I mean she was addicted to everything from sex to crystal-methamphetamine. What a waste!

That evening when she almost fell out of the truck, Annie was wearing tight white slacks, a denim top, and a bronze tan. She was attractive. They were probably at a pool hall drinking shots and scoring dope.

Sherry didn't know what to do. I thought following or watching Annie was really a waste of time and money. This is the question for grandparents: "Do I want custody? After all, I have already raised children, and I don't want to raise another one; not at my age." It's quite a dilemma. Sometimes I recommend to my clients to appear as if you are going to go for custody and bluff hoping they will straighten up. But for this to have any chance of working, you must really investigate, prepare your case, hire a lawyer, file in court for custody, and only pull out at the last possible moment. And even then it might not work.

It's still a commitment and it takes money and willpower. But in Annie's case, like many others, there was no hope. She was a mess. We needed a plan, an objective. Yes it did look like Sherry was a controller. Sherry hired me to watch her daughter destroy her grandson.

Sherry was paying for Annie's Scottsdale apartment. Annie rarely held a job. She lived on unemployment, welfare, or any aid she could muster through the government.

After watching Annie flounder that evening, I met with Sherry. I told her I would gladly watch Annie and Tommy because I needed to make a living. But I would prefer to work on a goal, an objective, a plan to solve the problem. I first asked who the father was. Sherry told me it was a guy who went to jail in the Midwest. According to Sherry, this guy had beaten Annie within an inch of her life and although Annie wouldn't testify against him, he had other criminal charges that landed him in the slammer. They lived together and Annie got pregnant and she moved or escaped to Arizona while he was in jail. The father hadn't ever seen his child. Sherry was already living in Arizona and Annie followed her mother for financial reasons. This is where the enabling continued.

Annie's track of decadence continued as well. She found the same crowd in Arizona that she had left in the Midwest. Her track of multiple partners, alcoholism, and drug addiction had blossomed again. These are things I look for and hope for in custody cases. Now it was time to document her lifestyle.

The only real hurdle was that Sherry didn't want custody, and bluffing Annie wouldn't work because she was an extreme case. Annie's problems were terminal and pathological. There was no way to straighten her out. I know a lot of people believe anything is possible and that nothing is hopeless. Well, I'm here to tell you the only hope for Annie and Tommy was adoption. In other words either the government steps in and takes the child for adoption or foster care, or Annie terminates her rights as a parent to Tommy by signing a release.

The options were interesting. If Annie agreed to adoption, the government wouldn't be involved—most likely. If Sherry filed a dependency action, then all hell would break loose. A dependency action is where the grandparents or a parent files an action in the juvenile court to have the government determine the children's best interests. When this happens the government generally appoints attorneys for the parties, including the children. A psychological evaluation begins and the psychologist will evaluate the parties to see where the children will live and with whom. Sometimes it's foster care because the government determines that nobody is fit to raise the children. Sometimes the children will ultimately live with more than one foster parent. This isn't really a good situation because the children will go from home to home and the problem of parenting isn't really solved. However, the parents still may maintain some parental rights or visitation.

In a private adoption in Arizona, the parents lose all rights and so do the grandparents. So if adoption is your only option, then you might want to locate somewhere where the new parents will share the child with you. In a perfect world, this could happen but it is rare. Legally in Arizona, once the child is adopted, that's it. The children are legally severed from the family.

I don't want to put down Sherry. She had spent thousands of dollars on Annie and Tommy. She was a concerned mother and grandmother. Unlike Annie, she had maternal instincts. Sherry had done everything she could. But Sherry had recently remarried since the death of her husband, and raising a child was not in the contract.

My plan worked. For two years on and off I had documented Annie's lifestyle. Now Tommy was five and because of frequent visits with his grandmother and uncle he was somehow doing all right. That was good and bad. The good part was he was progressing fairly normal. The bad part was how do you obtain custody without proving damage to the child? Answer: You don't. Unfortunately, judges, psychologists, and lawyers need to see damage before they react! The justice system is reactive.

Originally, when I took this case I recommended an intervention. The intervention would be to have all of Annie's brothers, mother, and grandmother who were still alive corner Annie and demand two things: That she needed to go through drug and alcohol rehabilitation, and that Tommy must live with his grandmother temporarily until Annie got on her feet.

Furthermore, Sherry wanted Annie to give her guardianship of Tommy. Of course Annie would be told this was temporary as well. Guardianship would make Sherry the legal parent of Tommy. Sherry, on my advice, already had an attorney prepare the guardianship papers. This was really the purpose of the intervention. I was hoping with all the family members present they could convince Annie to sign the papers then and there. This actually worked. Annie reluctantly signed the guardianship.

A week later, Annie moved into a halfway house. Annie read the Bible daily and began her rehabilitation. She did this for two months and then she got a job waiting tables. I told Sherry I feared she might start using again. Sherry agreed. So and I am not proud of this tactic, but I planted a spy in her restaurant. But before you jump to conclusions, it's not what you think. One evening when there were few people in the restaurant I sent in Alan[4], a counselor I knew from Alcoholics Anonymous. He sat in her section and ordered coffee. He was wearing an AA chain around his neck, in plain sight for Annie to see. It couldn't have worked better. Annie saw the chain and that evening he became her sponsor in AA. The only possible problem was he was loyal to Annie and not to me or Sherry even though he billed us for his services.

During this time, Sherry was looking for parents for Tommy. By going through a Christian organization she found a nice couple who wanted to love and raise Tommy. Most stories don't work out this well. Tommy really liked these people.

Annie appeared to be doing well so like a knucklehead Sherry let Tommy stay with Annie for a week. Frankly, Sherry's marriage was strained because of Tommy. Let's face it; he was a five-year-old boy with a lot of energy. But this was the straw that broke the camel's back. When Tommy came back he looked unhealthy. In a week's time, his

---

4.   Name has been changed to protect privacy

clock was all messed up. He had no regimen while he was at his mother's apartment.

When he went back to pre-school he pulled down his pants and showed little girls his penis. He also put his hand down one of the little girl's dress. How do you handle this? Sherry called a child psychologist who actually gave her some good advice. He said scold Tommy for what he did, but don't make a big deal out of it. Finally, we see a common sense approach to sex and children. Prosecutors and police detectives have told me the ordeal of interrogating children who have been molested is actually more detrimental than the act itself—granted within limitations.

We have no idea why Tommy did what he did. But the common denominator is Annie. Who knows what she watched or did in front of him with a man or a woman, but it was something. Now it was time for another intervention. This time I told Sherry she needed a social worker who could sell Annie on adoption. And of course this would terminate her parental rights.

Now as twisted as this sounds we were actually hoping Annie was using drugs and alcohol. We had no choice but to cut our losses. Chances were Annie was a lost cause.

What mother would sign away her child? I know of several cases when a college girl would get pregnant and would put the child up for adoption. The reason I am familiar with this scenario is because children have hired me to find their parents 20 years later. Those children who were adopted became adults and wanted to know who their parents are and why they were adopted. But generally speaking it is difficult to convince a mother to give up her child. And it is even more difficult when the child is no longer an infant. For all of Annie's problems, she still believed she had a bond with Tommy.

Sherry called a counselor from Christian Family Care. The counselor was good. She took a hard line approach to the situation with Annie. Sherry called and set up an appointment for all three of them. I went early and secretly taped the interview. I wanted to hear Annie's voice, hear her tone, and determine her progress or regress. Plus it would give Sherry some insight when playing back the tape for the next time, because we knew it wasn't over at this meeting.

Cindy[5], the counselor, tried to coerce Annie into giving up her son for adoption. The fact was Tommy hadn't lived with her in over a year. He really didn't miss his mother. And Annie had gone from a halfway house to an apartment. She had also worked at numerous restaurants waiting tables. There just wasn't any stability to Annie or her lifestyle. And I don't believe she wanted Tommy. If she had him, he would just be in her way. Annie was battling her problems of addiction every day. Finally after six months of hammering Annie every week, she finally agreed to terminate her rights to Tommy. She was naturally reluctant but she always believed she would still see her son and be a part of his life.

Now all we had to do was to find the father and terminate his rights. The term due-diligence comes to mind. Due-diligence is applied in law when you or an entity makes reasonable efforts to accomplish a given task.

In this example, I had to make reasonable efforts to locate Tommy's father, Craig[6]. Maybe he was still in jail or prison or maybe he was out and had started his own family. Nevertheless, being a detective or investigator, I had to start my investigation at the scene of the crime. I went to the county courthouse in Annie's hometown. I searched the records going back six years and found Craig's charges. I read through his criminal history and saw he was a real charmer. This guy had been convicted for concealed weapons charges,sexual battery, and bribing a juror.

The sexual battery charges were stemming from a girlfriend. Craig was convicted of holding a gun to her head while he put his penis in her mouth, and this wasn't role-playing. Craig had done this to Annie except he beat her afterwards and she spent two months in the hospital. This is a lesson in co-dependency because Annie got back together

---

5.   Name has been changed to protect privacy
6.   Name has been changed to protect privacy

with Craig-the-creep for a while afterward. Then he dumped her for the next victim—except the next one, unlike Annie, agreed to testify.

Justice wasn't really served by Craig because his sentence was only a year in the county jail. But we did the math—Craig had also been out for five years if he stayed straight. Craig's parents still lived in the same town. But Craig amazingly had married and moved to another state a few hundred miles away.

I located Craig and his new wife. But I decided to wait before I called him. I didn't want to spook the guy. If he was in fact the father, we had three options: If Craig was the father and wanted to terminate his rights, we would simply send him the paperwork and have him sign away Tommy. If he wanted to exercise his rights, we could fight him on the issues of desertion and abandonment. Although Annie went to drastic measures to keep away from Craig, Sherry's attorney believed because of his criminal history it was unlikely he could prevail and exercise his visitation. The final option was that if Craig wanted to be a father, he could pay his back child support to the tune of $30,000.

I really didn't think Craig would be excited about Tommy. Rather he would just sign the termination and sever his parental rights without a blood test. When I called Craig, he was actually excited to know he had a son. That's basically all I told him. I posed as an attorney and told him we were in Arizona and we believed his son was Tommy. A few days later he called back paranoid about the back child support. I felt like I was extorting him. If Craig wanted to exercise his parental rights it was going to cost him. He would have to fly to Arizona and hire an attorney. He would probably have to pay child support and, if he wanted visitation, he would have to pay Tommy's airfare.

He would also at some point have to establish paternity. He would probably need to hire an attorney and take a blood test to prove it was his child. But in all honesty we would object to Craig's visitation unless it was supervised because of his criminal and violent past. This actually transpired the way I thought it would. Craig was paranoid because it was evident he had spoken with an attorney regarding his rights and the consequences of exercising them. When Craig called back I asked for his address but he wouldn't give it to me. Needless to say I already had it. After all I'm the one who called him. Craig gave some attorney's name to mail the paperwork to. But because we had no proof an attorney was actually representing Craig we sent it to his home.

I wanted to use psychological warfare on this weasel. Besides he had used it on Annie and other women. I believe in strategy and I always consider the psychological aspect of the case, like how to manipulate the opponent from a psychological point of view! Maybe it wouldn't have made a difference, but a week later the termination was signed, sealed, and delivered.

This wasn't just another case for me. There were a lot of lives at stake. There are no guarantees. But to pat myself on the back a little, I went beyond what you can expect from a private investigator. I motivated Sherry as well as proposed some options and solutions while still keeping Tommy's best interest in mind. The other thing was we didn't have to fire a shot. There was no trial or expensive legal bills. There was only Tommy waiting and yearning for some real parents. Life is short and there are no guarantees. I hope Tommy lives a long and healthy life.

Child Protection Services and Government Agencies

This book wouldn't be complete without covering the government. With the government intruding on our basic rights today, it seems they are in our face in every component of our lives, from the IRS and our tax burden to deciding the future of our children.

I have interviewed psychologists, judges, police detectives, lawyers, teachers, and other experts in various fields. The conclusion is the government is assuming more and more control. The general consensus is most people resent the increasing restrictions on our personal freedoms. I have heard nothing good about CPS. They have been called Nazis and many other expletives by parents. Their complaints have been highly publicized. There are countless horror stories of CPS returning children to abusive parents and the end result is death. These stories are replete with beatings or hangings of young children who are too young to protect themselves. The complaint is children simply don't have rights. On the other hand, parents do.

Unfortunately, these rogue parents abuse the rights and their children. Children's rights could be another book. Some lobbying groups have sprouted throughout the country in an attempt to improve the legal rights of children. Again this has caused another controversy as well. Nobody seems to agree specifically what the children's rights should be and how they can be enforced. The laws may differ from state to state regarding parent's rights versus children's rights. The statutes are created and written by the legislature in your state.

I believe changes can be made to improve the legal system today, but the way disgruntled parents have gone about it is flawed. Professional lobbyists who have influence and expertise should be the commanders in this operation. Many parents or concerned citizens have not utilized this kind of organized plan for change. The parents are highly charged and emotional about their children but lack the direction and objectivity to accomplish the goal of protecting them.

You have fathers saying they get a bum rap in the courts while mothers say the law protects fathers who intimidate or fail to pay child support. Basic common sense has been thrown out the window regarding the future of children's lives. The fact is many parents aren't emotionally mature or stable enough to put aside their grievances from the divorce, so the children suffer. Although we all can agree that the children suffer, we can't seem to get past this in our own case. We see the destruction in other families but we lack the objectivity in ours.

The "me" generation has destroyed the American Family. Gangs have replaced the family unit and it won't get better for a long time. What the government ought to be building is plenty of prisons for children as well as for adults. Nobody has a sense of right and wrong. Yes, some things are gray, but a lot of things are still black and white and you can't wish them away. When does the truth hurt more than a lie?

In all the cases I have worked that have involved the government, I have seen very few times when the government did a good job. There simply isn't the incentive for them to find the truth. The anatomy or the legal gymnastics of involving the government in a custody case may differ from state to state. Typically it begins with a phone call from a concerned teacher, neighbor, doctor who has observed abuse. Then the Child Police or government investigates, though I don't know what they really do.

Some government agencies have counselors or caseworkers with credentials and some don't. I don't care what their credentials are. The bottom line should be that they are going to be an advocate of the child. In some states the laws are only written for the parents so the government is going to use the statutes or law to reunite the family. In other words very often they will investigate an allegation of abuse and place the child back into the family where the abuse occurred. This requires the least paperwork.

If they did their job, the parental rights may be terminated or the child may be placed with foster parents or a family member, or adopted.

Certainly not all the cases the government intervenes in are extreme cases. But a lot of them are. The standards for parenting for CPS are far different than the standards of many state courts. CPS is usually just happy when the children have a roof over their heads. But in state courts where people hire expensive lawyers, living conditions or lifestyle is paramount to awarding custody. These are two different playing fields, but they shouldn't be. The standards should be maintained if CPS was interested in the truth. I have worked cases where CPS returned the children to the parents after a "complete evaluation and investigation." Later we won custody in state court by proving the parents were unfit. Funny how CPS couldn't do that. Now who has the credentials?

Which brings us back to the reality that the government isn't interested in the truth. Quite the contrary. Their position is to reunite the family. In other words they want to tell parents how to parent. In some cases the government will make the parents take parenting classes and drug tests in hopes they can change their lives. It sounds like good intentions, but the percentage of parents who make it is low.

The Census Bureau reports there are more than four million grandparents raising their grandchildren today. How many fathers have custody? And how many fathers went to court to win custody? Or how many parents have joint custody? This changes on a daily basis because parents are going back to court regularly to amend the court orders.

The bottom line is young parents who the government tries to improve often fail. It's been my experience the government resents grandparents intervening in their children's parenting problems. But it's okay for the government to intervene or enable the bad parents to carry on their plight. I have seen cases where the Child Police try to dig dirt on the grandparents instead of focusing on the child who may be in jeopardy. The government simply resents the grandparents' involvement as part of the solution. But what I have told my clients is simple: If the Child Police give the parents in question a clean bill of health, the case isn't over. Quite the contrary, the case is just beginning.

But when I have worked for grandparents in this situation they get frustrated and depressed because they think the government can't see the problem. Actually they do see the problem, they just don't have the parenting standards or care standards you have. This is no reason to give up. In my opinion CPS employees are generally incompetent and lazy. They are not health care professionals, judges, lawyers, or even psychologists.

Now with them out of the way, you can proceed without their interference. I have seen very few cases where the judge values the opinion of a caseworker of CPS over an expert in private enterprise. So if several months down the line you are in court and the government shows up to say they've examined this case and their position is they are good parents, so what? Remember, they fail to do complete work.

In many cases I have worked, they have failed to point out criminal records or even previous evaluations completed by criminal psychologists regarding family background and deviant behavior. The old saying, "the fox watching the hen house" comes to mind. CPS may have its good points, but in my opinion you have to treat them just like police. If they want to interview you or evaluate you or your children or grandchildren, you need your attorney present or at least advice from your attorney. The meetings should be recorded so there is a record of the interview. Any allegation should have the burden of proof, meaning they need to prove the allegation. If the allegation benefits your position, then help with the investigation and find the truth. If it is detrimental to you, then prove it wrong. Remember, if the local police department is investigating the case, the burden of proof is from a criminal point of view. This means they need to prove the complaint beyond a shadow of a doubt. But CPS or the state courts will most likely not maintain that extreme of a standard. In other words, the allegation may stick with you in a custody case as the truth, even though the police fail to prosecute criminally.

When the government is investigating an allegation, you are not limited to their resources. Of course it may cost money to hire people, but you might want to hire your own attorney, doctor, or psychologist to dispute or prove an allegation. Too many people just assume the government or CPS has the final say. In some instances that's probably true. However, if you choose to fight the government or choose to pursue your case, hiring experts in private enterprise may be necessary to protect your reputation and children.

For those of you who can't afford an attorney it may be an option to obtain a court-appointed lawyer to represent you, your children, or your grandchildren. Nothing is perfect or foolproof, but if you are unaware of your options, let your fingers do the walking. There are court services, volunteer lawyers, and paralegal services available. Depending on where you live, a lot of these services may be free. Plus some people represent themselves in these cases. I don't recommend it, but when fighting for the future of your children, you need to pursue every option.

Some court services provide psychologists to evaluate the parents and children. These services are free and supported by tax dollars in your state. Bear in mind these services vary from state to state. CPS may be called something else in your state but it is usually a state organization. Bar associations for attorneys may also assist you in finding support groups, free legal services, or family attorney specialists. Caution: Some support groups are just lonely heart clubs whose members complain together over coffee or beer. These people are either not motivated to change anything or they are maybe ignorant of their options. Either way they may result in more hurt than help.

Unfortunately, the court system has become a contest for who can spend the most money. Without evidence people get crushed every day in the legal system because they run out of money. That's why I wrote this book. Some government services are better than nothing when you have no money. But solid evidence in custody cases shifts the balance of power.

In conclusion, government agencies or services can help, but they can also hinder depending on the situation. Remember, the government is overworked and rarely thorough. The same applies when you hire an attorney. You must get involved to ensure your story is told or that you maximize the child's best interest in a given case.

Can Fathers Win Custody?

I know that a lot of people reading this book are going to think I wrote it for men. But I didn't. I wrote this book for parents and grandparents and anyone who can or should achieve the goal of custody. The fact is there are a lot of bad parents in America no matter what their sex happens to be. But I have also found that generally fathers have a disadvantage in custody disputes. This may be for many reasons. To me the reasons are irrelevant because I am interested in helping parents and grandparents who deserve to attain custody no matter the sex.

Over the years I have spoken to fathers' rights groups and grandparents' rights groups. When I spoke to fathers' groups I found many common denominators. Some of the fathers said the system has destroyed their ability to have a relationship with their child. Many of them received bad advice and a lot of them did not get involved in their cause. Almost all of them wanted the laws to change for fathers' rights. Their solution was to have a 50/50 split of custody for all parents. They actually believe that would be the best solution. If this law were passed, then all the fathers I have helped achieve custody would be losers and so would their children. Unfortunately, because most of these fathers have never won custody, they have bought into this. Of course, their comeback would be that "few fathers ever win, so we still believe in a 50/50 split.

Let's play the "what if" game for a minute. What if the mother is a drug addict? Should she have a 50/50 split? I think not. What if the mother is mentally ill? What if she is an alcoholic? In fact, many parents today are either on prescription drugs, illegal drugs, or have an alcohol problem.

Why are they on these mood-altering devices? That's an easy one: Because the drugs are a symptom of another problem. The drugs just simply treat the symptoms instead of treating the real problem. Sometimes there is no cure for a parent with psychological difficulties. So I ask you, should parents automatically—by law—have equal time with their children? Equal time with a heroine addict is not in the best interest of a child! But because the system is slanted in favor of mothers, there are a lot of fathers who believe they have no chance in custody disputes. One evening I spoke for an hour explaining to them how to take charge of their cases and gather evidence. Afterward I had fathers tell me they were very impressed by my information and me. Some of these fathers were attorneys, police officers, and pilots—one was even a therapist. But they said the father I had brought with me who had won sole custody of his child when the child was 15 months old impressed them. In fact, the father had not even been married to the mother and still won sole custody. The group thought this kind of result was unheard of. I told them this was my most celebrated victory in child custody because my client was my own brother! Still, the fathers' group did not understand why my brother had won.

He won because we employed the tactics I have outlined in this book. We set a goal of custody and worked tirelessly on a strategy to win the case. This is something these fathers did not understand. In fact, there are few attorneys and parents out there who actually understand how to win a custody case. Because I have dealt with this in my family, I understand how emotional and difficult custody disputes are. Again, if courts awarded all parents a 50/50 split, my brother would not have sole custody. (For more on this case, see "The Combat Mindset" in Part 1.)

Yes, it is true fathers often do not get a fair shake in custody. That's why it is so important for them to prepare and educate themselves about this subject. Custody should be awarded by the merits of the case. The problem is there are a lot of fathers who have been fed erroneous baloney by some of these fathers' groups. They have been told they can't have custody. Even their own attorneys tell them they can't have custody. My results speak for themselves and there are more and more fathers winning custody today. But it takes intestinal fortitude to achieve custody.

X COMMANDMENT
IT IS NEVER OVER

Your case is never over. You may be fighting for parental rights in your case for years. That's why I tell my clients that even after the trial and custody is decided, it still might be temporary. Some parents cannot get along no matter what the outcome of the custody battle is. So don't let your guard down—you may need to continue your investigation and preparation of the facts in your case.

0-595-33656-6

7818798R0

Made in the USA
Lexington, KY
17 December 2010